AARON KHERIATY
ON LIFE, FAITH, AND LEADERSHIP

TEPEYAC LEADERSHIP SERIES

AARON KHERIATY
ON LIFE, FAITH, AND LEADERSHIP

TEPEYAC LEADERSHIP SERIES

TLI
PUBLISHING
Phoenix, AZ

About the Tepeyac Leadership Series

Tepeyac Leadership, Inc. (TLI) is a nonprofit organization dedicated to civic leadership development for lay Catholic professionals around the globe. The Tepeyac Leadership Series is part of TLI's mission to deliver civic leadership development to lay Catholics in the U.S. and beyond. TLI offers a catalyst development experience that equips lay Catholics to become virtuous leaders, influence the culture and serve the common good. Learn more at TLIprogram.org.

The editor, Laurie Strom is a Deacon's wife, grandmother, and a former Executive VP & COO of SAE Industry Technologies Consortia and Honeywell Aerospace Director, where she managed engineering teams in multiple countries. Now she is a mentor, coach, writer, and photographer - praising God and finding science and faith beautifully intertwined. There is beauty in a job well done.

Assistant Editor, Julie Bernhard, TLI 2025 Cohort

Cover Design: Maria Fernanda Hernandez

Dedication

This book is dedicated to the first eight cohorts of the TLI program - 2018 through 2025. May they continue to deepen their faith, prosper in their professional pursuits, and become the virtuous leaders they are meant to be.

"O Mother, strengthen the faith of our brothers and sisters in the laity, so that in every field of social, professional, cultural and political life, they may act in accordance with the truth and the law brought by your son to mankind." (St. John Paul II 1979)

Hail Mary
St. Juan Diego, Pray for us.

TABLE OF CONTENTS

(para. x) indicates the applicable paragraph number.

TABLE OF CONTENTS (CONT.)

(para. x) indicates the applicable paragraph number.

TABLE OF CONTENTS (CONT.)

(para. x) indicates the applicable paragraph number.

FOREWORD

A Time To Be Courageous

Aaron Kheriaty once made me promise never to tell anyone that he had helped me with the scientific and medical research for my 2018 book *When Harry Became Sally: Responding to the Transgender Moment.*[1] The world was crazy back then, with cancel culture in full swing, and Aaron was rightly concerned that he would lose his job as a professor at the University of California-Irvine (UCI) Medical School if anyone found out he had helped on a project that transgender activists would claim was "anti-trans." This was *California*, after all. Aaron wasn't a coward. But he knew that courage had two opposing vices - cowardice on one side and foolhardiness on the other. It would have been foolhardy, not courageous, at the time for him to lose his job, especially with a wife and five kids who depended on his salary and benefits. He could make his largest contributions to exposing the scandal that is so-called "gender affirming care" behind the scenes, by equipping others who had the job security to enter into the public square.

Of course, the irony of all ironies is that the University of California did eventually fire Aaron, and it was over a contested question of medical ethics. But what did him in was his opposition to experimental vaccines and their mandates. And again here, Aaron wasn't being foolhardy in his opposition - but as a medical doctor who cared for patients with Covid-19, as an ethicist who chaired the University of California's Ethics Committee, and as a professor who served as a moral role model to students, he had to take a public stance against what he viewed as an injustice and violation of medical ethics, that he was being asked to - forced to - directly participate in.

Now, why was Aaron willing and able to take such a public stance, knowing that it might cost him everything? Aaron had spent well over two decades by that point in his own moral formation in the virtues and intellectual formation in medicine. I first met Aaron in 2010 at a gathering at Princeton University. We were both working

---

[1] New York: Encounter Books, 2018.

on a project examining the adverse social costs of pornography sponsored by the Witherspoon Institute.[2] At that time, he was a young psychiatrist just a few years out of residency training. I recognized in him a kindred spirit, someone who wanted to place his intellect at the service of society in fidelity to the Church. We struck up a friendship and began collaborating on various projects.

A few years later, I was working on a large report for the Heritage Foundation on physician assisted suicide[3]. In that report, I drew upon Aaron's work as a psychiatrist situating doctor assisted suicide in the context of broader suicide prevention efforts, and his research on the social contagion effects of suicide. Our professional research on various issues in bioethics continued to run in parallel. When, just a few years later, I started my research into transgender issues, Aaron helped me tremendously in understanding the science and the medicine. Aaron had been working for several years on background research for a report published in *The New Atlantis* on sexuality and gender, and he had a solid grasp of the scientific research.[4] I learned much from our collaborations together on these projects and found I could trust Aaron's judgment on these challenging and controversial issues. It's a true shame that students at UCI's medical school no longer get the benefit of his wisdom.

After he lost his job at the medical school, I immediately came to his defense with an article in *Newsweek* titled, "Why I'm Pro-Vaccine but Anti-Vaccine Mandate," where I explained: "Dr. Kheriaty and I made different decisions about the Covid vaccination.... We can protect the most vulnerable without forcing the vaccine on those who conscientiously object. We can be both pro-vaccine and anti-

---

[2] Layden, Mary Anne, and Mary Eberstadt. *The Social Costs of Pornography: A Statement of Findings and Recommendations.* Princeton, NJ: Witherspoon Institute, 2010.

[3], "Always Care, Never Kill: How Physician-Assisted Suicide Endangers the Weak, Corrupts Medicine, Compromises the Family, and Violates Human Dignity and Equality," March 14, 2015, available at **https://www.heritage.org/health-care-reform/report/always-care-never-kill-how-physician-assisted-suicide-endangers-the-weak**

[4] Mayer, Lawrence S., and Paul R. McHugh. *Sexuality and Gender: Findings from the Biological, Psychological, and Social Sciences.* Special Report, The New Atlantis, no. 50 (Fall 2016): 4–116.

vaccine mandate."[5] When Aaron was fired from the university, I was pleased to bring him on board to direct the bioethics program at the think tank where I serve as president, the Ethics and Public Policy Center (EPPC). Now, he has the job security that he lacked in the academy, free to tell the fullness of truth in the public square.

Since joining EPPC, Aaron has continued his valuable research on issues ranging from abortion and assisted reproductive technologies to reform of our federal public health agencies - after all, there's a reason the Biden administration instructed Twitter to censor him. I continue to be impressed by the willingness to tackle thorny issues, stepping into public controversies to speak the truth with clarity and conviction. We need models of faithful Catholics in public life, people who are not afraid to step into the breach and speak courageously. Aaron has a supple mind, with wide-ranging interests across multiple disciplines. His deep reading in medicine, philosophy, theology, political theory, history, and sociology allows for his unique ability to produce interdisciplinary scholarship and commentary on the issues that matter most. In this interview, Aaron describes some of the people and ideas that have influenced him, sharing his keen insights on life, faith, and leadership.

By Ryan T. Anderson, Ph.D.
President of the Ethics and Public Policy Center

---

[5] December 21, 2021. https://www.newsweek.com/why-im-pro-vaccine-anti-vaccine-mandate-opinion-1661472.

INTRODUCTION

I think God needs a handful of people in every sector of society to help establish the peace of Christ in the kingdom of Christ. And so, it doesn't matter if you're a street sweeper or a surgeon; God needs you there, wherever you're called, and you need to have a sense of responsibility that you're doing something great. (para. 263)

The Tepeyac Leadership Series aims to provide inspiration and insights for Catholics based on contemporary models of lay Catholic leadership. The objective of the book series and its intended focus is to showcase exemplary lay Catholic leaders. This book features Aaron Kheriaty, a Fellow and Director of the Program in Bioethics and American Democracy at the Ethics and Public Policy Center.

In an engaging question-and-answer interview format between Aaron and Laurie Strom, editor for TLI Publishing, Aaron shares from his own life the surprises and challenges God had in store for him on the journey of his vocation - going from a charmed childhood in Bellingham, Washington, to the discovery of the Catholic intellectual tradition at the University of Notre Dame, to med school and Ethics Committees, to court cases and advocating for sound public policies. *Aaron Kheriaty: on life, faith, and leadership* seeks to capture the dance of a soaring kite, a brilliant philosophic mind guided by faith and the science of psychiatry. It was born out of admiration and desire to inspire future generations through Aaron's example.

The book is structured to give the reader an insight into three concrete areas: the life, faith, and leadership of Aaron Kheriaty. With the aid of the table of contents, readers may jump into the area or questions they want to learn about first and explore the rest at their own pace. The text remains true to the conversation with Aaron, but some of the questions have been modified to provide a smoother transition between topics. All proceeds from the sale of the book go to funding the mission of TLI.

Thank you for your interest in the life of Aaron Kheriaty, your support of TLI and the time you will dedicate to reading this book. We hope you find in its pages much inspiration to nurture your own life, faith, and leadership.

Part 1
Life

The teachings of Saint Josemaría Escrivá, the formation I've received, and Opus Dei have been a very significant influence on my life.
(para. 31)

[Hippocratic Society is] an attempt to have a medical society that is dedicated to the proposition that medicine should be aimed always, and only, at healing. Things that are contrary to healing - reshaping the human body, euthanizing someone at their request, killing an unborn child - these things don't have a rightful place in medicine.
(para. 118)

---

1. Laurie: *Thank you, Aaron, for being with us today to discuss life, faith, and leadership. Let's begin with your childhood history and earliest memories. Where were you born, and how many people were in your family?*

2. Aaron: I was born in Bellingham, Washington, and I grew up with a sister who was one year older and a brother who was five years younger. My father worked as a computer programmer, first at the University in Bellingham, and then he developed his own software company in the early days of computers and software. He was a pioneer. My mother was a stay-at-home mom. Then, she helped part-time with the family software business. When my younger brother was in high school, she went back to school and got a master's degree in counseling. She started doing clinical counseling and, eventually, school counseling.

3. My parents were faithful Catholics, and I'm very grateful that I was baptized as an infant and raised Catholic - given the sacraments, sent to Catholic school (K – 8), and taught in the home how to pray. My father is now a permanent deacon. He retired from the software business a couple of decades ago and discerned that he was called to

the diaconate. He serves the Archdiocese of Seattle as a deacon - still at the home parish where I grew up.

4. I had a wonderful childhood. It was really charmed. I grew up on a lake, and so I was sort of amphibious. I spent summers in the water and on the ski boat, wakeboarding, water skiing, and swimming. I had friends that lived on the lake. We could hang out together and bus from one house to another on ski boats. It was really wonderful! I spent the winters snow skiing up in the mountains. Bellingham was a beautiful place to fall in love with the outdoors and find God in nature.

5. I did some great hiking and backpacking trips when I was in high school, which gave me a real love for the beauty of being on the water and being up in the mountains. We would vacation in the San Juan Islands with my extended family on a boating trip every summer. I just had so many blessings as a child.

6. I have a wonderful older sister and younger brother. We argued more as kids, but we're very close now. Typical sibling stuff. We went to a public high school. There was no Catholic high school in town, so we didn't have that option. Then, I moved away from Bellingham at the age of eighteen to go to college.

7. No one has a perfect childhood, but mine was pretty close. As a psychiatrist, I treat so many people who suffered as children, sometimes tremendously, sometimes with unspeakable horrors and evils in the form of abuse and neglect. Every day, I'm grateful that I came from an intact family with two parents who love each other. No marriage is perfect, but they [my parents] clearly loved each other and were totally devoted to us. They were very generous and showed us how to serve. I see so many people in my clinical practice who don't have that: people who came from broken homes and people who experienced horrible forms of child abuse, sometimes at the hands of family members. They can certainly find God in those crosses and in that suffering, but I feel sort of charmed and blessed to have had a stable and healthy childhood.

8. When I was a senior in high school, my future wife moved from California, where she grew up, to Bellingham, where I lived. Her father got a job there [in Bellingham]. We met and started dating

right away. I dated her my senior year, which is not what I was expecting that year. I wasn't looking to establish a relationship or to have a girlfriend. I just wanted to finish high school, graduate, and, you know, get out of town. Growing up in a medium-sized town was great, but I wanted to go off to college somewhere else and experience the world. I was very much focused on getting into college and wrapping up high school. And then I met Jennifer, and we fell in love.

9. We ended up going to different colleges that were in the same state, not by design. I went to the University of Notre Dame, and she went to Indiana University (IU). When we met, she actually knew that she wanted to go to IU to study music. That's where her music teacher had gone and recommended that she go. I knew I wanted to go to Notre Dame because they had a great football team.

10. Laurie: *It's been a good year for your team!*

11. Aaron: Yes, they had a good year this year!

12. We [Jennifer and I] ended up in the same state but dated long-distance for four years in college. We got engaged the summer before our senior year of college and got married right after we both graduated. I ended up marrying my high school sweetheart!

13. And then, right after we got married, her father got another job down here where she grew up. They moved back, literally, to the same street where she grew up - a different house, but the same street.

14. Laurie: *And when you say here, where do you mean?*

15. Aaron: She grew up in Dana Point, California, which is in Orange County, and we now live in San Juan Capistrano, which is the town right next door to Dana Point. Her parents still live on the street where she grew up. Her father had to move a long way for five years to marry her off. [Just kidding!] But we all ended up back here in California, which is now my home. I've lived here longer than anywhere else and consider myself, for better or worse, a Californian now.

16. I'm still fond of Washington. It's a beautiful place. I don't miss the rain. I like the sunshine here in California, but we get up there [Bellingham] once or twice a year. My parents still live on that lake where I grew up. It's a great place to go with our kids in the summer and have them experience some of that joy of being on the water and swimming and skiing and inner tubing and all that. All that stuff that I did as a kid.

17. Laurie: *Speaking of your family, how many children do you have?*

18. Aaron: I have five boys and no girls. The oldest just graduated from the University of Dallas (UD). He married a girl that he met at UD, and they had their first baby in November. I don't have any daughters, but they had a little girl - so I have a granddaughter now, which is just wonderful! They live in Dallas.

19. The next oldest is a junior at the University of Dallas studying politics. Then we have one who is a senior in high school, another who's a freshman in high school, and the youngest is in seventh grade. So, thirteen to twenty-four is the age range of the five boys.

20. Laurie: *Wow! That's an active household.*

21. Aaron: Yes. It's high energy. We still have three at home. They eat a lot, and they make messes, and it's sometimes loud, but it's great.

22. Laurie: *Wonderful! It sounds like they are enjoying life like you did growing up!*

23. *Let's talk now about some of the people who were most influential in your early life. Was it parents, or teachers, or clergy? Who really had an influence on you growing up?*

24. Aaron: First and foremost, my parents were examples of faith for me, and they helped me develop a sense of responsibility, work ethic, and a desire to excel in school. They always supported my pursuits.

25. Starting in seventh grade through high school, I swam competitively and would have to get up at 4:45 in the morning to make it to swim practice on time. God bless my Dad! He would wake up that early and bring me every day to swim practice. He never

complained. He would drop me off, and then there was a track next door, so he would go jog or walk on the track. It's still dark outside very early in the morning!

26. They [my parents] showed total dedication to their children and helping us pursue school, or athletics, or other extracurriculars. They got us into piano lessons early, and my brother and sister had more musical talent than I did. They stuck with it longer, but I was at least exposed to that as a child. So, my parents were certainly the most influential people in my life.

27. For the first eighteen years, I had some good pastors at our parish. The pastor who was there when I was in high school, really gave me a sense of needing to learn how to pray and develop personal piety beyond just attending the sacraments. He was a very good man. He passed away recently. In the last years of his life, he was dealing with ALS, Lou Gehrig's disease, and the long and difficult decline that goes along with that. But he continued serving as a pastor at another parish until he died. I think he was a great witness of a man who carried the cross that our Lord gave him. Father Jim Lee was his name.

28. I had some youth group leaders that were influential, too, including a Protestant Young Life Group that I did some activities with at summer camp and some backpacking trips. They were good mentors for me, young men who were trying to be faithful to Christ and loved the Word of God.

29. When I got to college, I was very fortunate to discover the Catholic intellectual tradition. I had some very good professors at Notre Dame, where I studied philosophy and pre-medical sciences. In philosophy, I was fortunate to study with a great Thomist, Ralph McInerny, who also passed away a few years ago. I studied with another Thomist, Alfred Freddoso and we read the Summa. David Solomon was another professor there who taught me the history of ethics. He founded the Center for Ethics and Culture at Notre Dame while I was there, and he also passed away recently. So, I had some wonderful philosophy professors who introduced me to the Catholic intellectual tradition.

30. I also had some wonderful friends. I had three college roommates that are still some of my best friends. We try to get together every couple of years. We roomed together for the first three years. Two of them are now priests. One is a priest in the Archdiocese of Wyoming, the other is a priest in the Archdiocese of Chicago, and the third is married with children. One of them, when I was a freshman, retaught me how to pray the Rosary. He had a great devotion to Our Lady. I knew the basic prayers, but I was not in the habit of praying it. I remember him asking me one day if I wanted to pray the Rosary and get a little coaching from him. [I agreed], "Okay, which of the beads and how do I do this?" Wonderful guys who were normal, very engaged, fun, and very social college students, but also had a life of prayer and piety. That was a great example for me.

31. I also met some guys at Notre Dame who were involved at the Opus Dei Center. I started attending means of formation there for men and that helped me tremendously. The director of the center, Jeff Langan, who's now a priest of Opus Dei, was very helpful. Spiritual direction was very helpful from a priest of Opus Dei, Father Jerry Kolf, who ended up presiding at my wedding. The teachings of Saint Josemaría Escrivá, the formation I've received, and Opus Dei have been a very significant influence on my life. I was fortunate to encounter that in college while I was at Notre Dame. Then, in my senior year, I was able to live at the Opus Dei Center near campus. It was a great experience for me to have a community life with other people who are trying to pursue holiness in their everyday lives, offer their work and their studies up to God, and sanctify their ordinary work.

32. So, college was a great experience. I know many people in college tend to drift from the faith, or maybe they stopped practicing for a while, but I was fortunate to come into contact with friends right away who encouraged me in my faith and professors who helped me dig into the Catholic intellectual tradition. And then, means of formation like retreats and days of recollection at the Opus Dei Center helped me develop a life of prayer, a deeper appreciation for the sacraments, and a desire to really serve God in my personal life, in my family life, and in my professional work.

33. Laurie: *That gives us great hope for college!*

34. Aaron: Yes!

35. Laurie: *Did you have a feeling that you were going to specialize in bioethics when you went to med school, or how did that evolve?*

36. Aaron: That's a good question. I did a little bit. I liked science. I always had in the back of my mind, "Maybe I'll be a physician." I had friends in high school who told me, "Hey, you'd be a good doctor!" I could imagine being a family doctor, a physician. I had some very good science teachers in high school; the humanities teaching I got at the public high school was relatively weak, but the science teaching I got was very good. So I developed an interest in science and discovered philosophy kind of by accident at Notre Dame. I started out as a science major, and then you have to take two courses in philosophy and two courses in theology there. My Intro to Philosophy course just fascinated me.

37. Then I discovered I could do a pre-professional degree where I got my pre-med requirements and combined those with a humanities degree. Notre Dame had that option, and so for me, studying both philosophy and pre-med was a great kind of balance. I really loved philosophy, and I could see myself as an academic philosopher. I considered going to graduate school in philosophy and also applying to medical school.

38. What ended up happening was that I was dating Jennifer at the time and talking about which direction I wanted to go in. At that point, we were talking about the possibility of marriage in the future. She made a very good suggestion, "Look, if you study philosophy, you're only going to be able to do philosophy. There's a limited number of jobs and a limited number of schools. We'll have to live, and you'll have to work wherever you happen to get a decent position, hopefully, a tenure-track position, but it might be someplace where we wouldn't have otherwise chosen to settle down. Whereas, if you study medicine, you can always do medical ethics. You can always pursue your philosophical interests in that context, but you'll have a lot more flexibility. That's maybe more of a 'Both/And' proposition." She turned out to be right. So, I said, "Okay, I'll apply to medical school, and if I get in I'll go, but I'll continue to pursue medical ethics." That was my attitude.

39. I ended up getting into a couple of schools, but I picked Georgetown because we like the city; we like DC. But also, there was a bioethicist, a Catholic layman named Dr. Edmund Pellegrino, who was very well respected - sort of one of the founding fathers of American bioethics. He served for a time as the chairman of the President's Council for Bioethics. He was very well-regarded in the field and well-published. He was a physician as well, and I thought, "Wouldn't it be great to go and try to get some mentoring from Dr. Pellegrino?" He was the kind of physician-ethicist I would want to be.

40. When I arrived at Georgetown, I immediately arranged to meet with him [Dr. Pellegrino] and he was very gracious. He was a real gentleman and a scholar, which is kind of cliché, but he *was* a complete gentleman and a scholar! He sat down with me; he listened to this wide-eyed kid talking about my interest in science and ethics and encouraged me to get everything I could from medical school, "Everything you're going to study here is important." Then, as I proceeded through my training, he took me under his wing in my fourth year. I did some ethics research with him and presented a paper at the Ethics Center that he ran. He did become a very helpful mentor while I was there, which was great!

41. I considered doing an MD/PhD and getting the PhD in ethics. As I was going through the process of applying for that, we had our first child. I was a second-year medical student. That [MD/PhD] would have extended my training by another five, maybe six years. Jennifer sort of gently nudged me and said, "Look, we got residency after this. At some point, you're going to have to get a job and start making an income." So I wisely discerned that I could keep up on ethics as a physician. I could get involved in the Ethics Committee, which I did there [at Georgetown] and during residency [at UC Irvine]. I continued reading and studying and I continued doing ethics research in med school and residency. With the MD and that kind of experience, I wouldn't necessarily need a formal degree in bioethics in order to engage in that work. She [Jennifer] was right about that. Actually, that's exactly what happened!

42. I maintained my interest in ethics. I continued in my residency to do research and writing on ethics. I joined the Ethics Committee in residency and continued as an early faculty member. You know, if

you stay on a committee long enough, eventually they make you chair of the committee!

43. I ended up chairing the Ethics Committee at the University of California (UC) Irvine, where I did residency and then joined the faculty after residency. Gradually, as my career at UC Irvine developed, I did more and more ethics. During my first year as a faculty member, maybe fifteen percent of my time was devoted to ethics, and by the time I left the University in 2021, it was about 50/50 - working in teaching, research, and administrative work in psychiatry, and the other half teaching, research, and administrative work in ethics. So my career evolved and developed in precisely the direction I was hoping for when I was an undergraduate, but did not know how to put that together. God, in his providence, was very good to me, and it all worked out. Jennifer's advice was great, "Go pursue your MD. That will give you some degree of credibility if you're talking about clinical ethics and you're trying to deal with physicians on an ethics committee or a hospital setting."

44. So here I am. After I left the University, I established a private practice, which is now about 15-20 hours a week, and the rest of my time is continuing to do research, writing and working on ethics and public policy. I've done that combination of work for about twenty years, if you include residency at the University of California, Irvine. Now, I'm doing it in an independent think tank/independent research institute and a private practice setting. It's been a great career where I've been able to pursue both of those interests: medicine and science on the one hand, and ethics and philosophy on the other hand.

45. **Laurie:** *So, that think tank - is that the Ethics and Public Policy Center [eppc.org] where you are a director?*

46. **Aaron:** Yes, I'm the director. It's called The Bioethics and American Democracy Program at the Ethics and Public Policy Center. So that's my official title today.

47. **Laurie:** *But you also have a practice?*

48. **Aaron:** I have a private practice in psychiatry, just an outpatient practice - general adult psychiatry. So I treat patients part-time as well.

49. Laurie: *Nice. Keeping that dual career approach going - smart!*

50. Aaron: And I think it's important as a clinical ethicist that I'm a practicing physician as well. That kind of keeps my feet on the ground. It's possible when you're doing philosophy or ethics to get lost in abstractions or in sometimes arcane academic disputes. Philosophy has that tendency to maybe float off into the ether. So being a practicing physician has really been good for me, keeping my feet on the ground in the concrete, kind of messy, realities of patients' lives and day-to-day clinical practice.

51. Laurie: *That makes sense!*

52. *Going back to ethics and public policy, can you share with us a little about the principle of informed consent? How is it derived from an understanding of faith and ethics? How does it relate to the court cases UC Irvine and Missouri that you are a plaintiff in, and what is the status of those court cases?*

53. Aaron: The principle of informed consent is grounded in, and certainly consistent with, the principle in Catholic Social Teaching known as the dignity of the human person: Man is created in the image and likeness of God with an intellect and free will that needs to be given respect and regard. Anything that would involve undue coercion, especially regarding the bodily integrity of the person, would potentially violate that principle.

54. The principle of informed consent sort of came to prominence in the 20th century in medical ethics, starting with the Nuremberg Code, which is a response to the Nazi atrocities in World War II and the experiments that were done on death camp prisoners by Nazi physicians. The world responded to those with horror, even though the Nazi physicians mounted arguments in their defense [which] we need to look at, contend with and take seriously. They said these people were going to die anyway. They said that the conditions in the camp were so horrible that many of the prisoners actually wanted to be on the medical wards because they got slightly better food, clothing, shelter, and slightly better treatment than the ones in the general camp. And those things were actually true, as disturbing as that is, but that still didn't justify the fact that these people were

forced to participate in unconsented experiments and, in many cases, harmed or even killed in order to try to glean scientific information.

55. One of the disturbing things about that is that we actually did glean useful scientific information. There's this stereotype that the Nazi doctors were just sort of opportunistic sadists that wanted to torture prisoners in the name of science. A few of them probably fell into that category. But the disturbing fact is, there's still information found in medical textbooks that was gleaned from these experiments. It's an ethical question: What do you do with that information? Should we at least acknowledge its source and acknowledge that the experiments done to discover this information should never have been done? This is one example: We know how long it takes for a fertilized ovum to traverse from the fallopian tube, where fertilization takes place, and implant in the uterus. It takes three to four days. How do we know that? Because Nazi doctors vivisected pregnant women to discover that finding. But you could find that [information] in any embryology textbook or any obstetrics textbook today.

56. So, the world reacted to this quite rightly with horror, and there were a dozen Nazi doctors that were tried at Nuremberg. About half of them were convicted, and a few of those were even sentenced to death by hanging. Then, the Nuremberg tribunal produced something called the Nuremberg Code. The very first principle of the Nuremberg Code is the principle of informed consent. That became sort of the bulwark and the guiding principle for the ethics of human subjects research following World War II. Then, in the 1960s and 1970s, it started being applied to the clinical setting as well. Now, it's instantiated in laws related to medicine, laws related to human subjects research, and federal guidelines on human subjects research. Individuals have the right, after being informed of the risks, benefits, and alternatives to a proposed treatment or proposed experimental intervention, to accept or decline that intervention and to opt out of an experiment at any point. They can withdraw consent at any point in the process, and that has to be respected, even if we could get better, more useful, or more complete data by forcing people to stay in an experiment that they already enrolled in.

57. So, that was the principle I saw being violated by the Covid-19 vaccine mandates. The argument for violating it was, [paraphrasing]

"Well, it may not benefit the recipient if they're at low risk of harm from Covid, but it might benefit other people." There was sort of a social solidarity argument, which is also a principle of Catholic Social Teaching, but I found that argument, in this case, to be remarkably weak because we knew very early on that these vaccines did not stop infection or transmission of the virus. The traditional principle of informed consent in medical ethics should have applied in my case, and I made the case in the courts [*Kheriaty v. Drake*] when I challenged the University of California's vaccine mandate. I ended up losing that case, although ironically, the case against the University probably would prevail if I filed it today. Subsequent to the ruling in my case, the Ninth Circuit, which is the circuit court above the District Court where I filed my case, came out with a ruling basically endorsing the argument of my case, which was: We now know that these do not stop infection and transmission of the virus. Therefore, the 1905 precedent, *Jacobson v. Massachusetts* related to a smallpox vaccine, doesn't actually apply to the Covid shots because they're not analogous in that way.

58. Laurie: *Have you thought about appealing it?*

59. Aaron: It's too late to appeal. Unfortunately, there's a statute of limitations; there's a time limit as to how long you can wait before you appeal. So it would be too late to appeal that case, and I'm not really inclined to file another case because I'm not sure there's any point anymore. I don't see the University [at UC Irvine] actually mandating the vaccine again.

60. The other case, the censorship case, the *Missouri v. Biden* case, does not necessarily directly deal with the principle of informed consent, although I was censored when I was trying to explain this principle to people. The first instance I noticed censorship was an interview with Alison Morrow, who's a former CBS journalist who had left journalism, at least as a full-time job, and was working doing film for the Department of Natural Resources in the State of Washington. But she had a podcast that she did out of her home. So I went on her podcast. I talked about the ethics of vaccine mandates, and I talked about my case. That was censored on YouTube; she ended up losing her YouTube account for a period of time. Then her employer said, [paraphrasing] "You need to take down the interview with Aaron, or we're going to fire you." She refused, and they fired

her. So she has a case against the State of Washington, which I anticipate she will win because that was a clear First Amendment, free speech [issue], and she worked for the government. Perhaps a private employer could have decided they wanted to fire her based on viewpoint discrimination, or whatever, but the State, I think, can't do that. So, she has a case in court.

61. That instance of censorship became part of the evidence that I submitted in *Missouri v. Biden*. This case is still in the District Court. We went to the Supreme Court, which did not uphold the preliminary injunction based on a technicality related to standing. [Now] we're back at the District Court and the government is proposing a settlement, so it looks like we will get at least some of what we were pursuing in that case.

62. Laurie: *Please refresh my memory. What's the background of that case?*

63. Aaron: That case involves the State of Missouri and Louisiana, and five private plaintiffs, of which I am one. Dr. Jay Bhattacharya, the new director of the NIH [National Institute of Health], was another plaintiff in that case; he has recused himself since his appointment to the government post. Basically, we're alleging that the federal government was pressuring and coercing social media companies to censor disfavored information.

64. The evidence we submitted was mostly related to censorship during Covid of people who are challenging the government's preferred pandemic policies. Jay and Dr. Martin Kulldorff, one of our other plaintiffs, were arguing that lockdowns and prolonged school closures were going to do more harm than good and, on balance, not a good public health approach. They were censored. We now know that they were censored by the former NIH Director and by Anthony Fauci; we have internal emails calling for a "swift and devastating" takedown of [Jay and Martin's] arguments, as they put it.

65. What we found on discovery is actually censorship on all kinds of other issues as well: there was election-related censorship, there was censorship on abortion, there was censorship on gender ideology, there was censorship on people criticizing US monetary policy and people criticizing US foreign policy. The censorship

apparatus started being built around 2017, and it ramped up massively during Covid. But it was in place prior to that, so the range of issues that Americans were censored on was pretty vast. I think we pretty much won the argument that this was happening. Mark Zuckerberg went on Joe Rogan's Podcast, and he also wrote a letter to Jim Jordan, who is chairing the Weaponization of Government Committee in the House of Representatives. Zuckerberg basically admitted, [paraphrasing] "Yes, the government was pressuring us to censor, and we tried to resist for a while, but they beat us down. We finally gave in, and we shouldn't have done that. I regret doing that." Which is essentially the argument that we made in our case and what we've presented to the court.

66. Donald Trump signed an executive order on Day One in office, basically saying that he would investigate and dismantle the government's censorship apparatus. J.D. Vance talked about this issue during his Vice Presidential Debate with Tim Walz. The case kind of put the issue on the map politically. The evidence that we've uncovered in the case has made it clear, and then we have the CEO of Facebook basically admitting that this happened. Elon Musk has also admitted that this happened. In fact, he allowed some independent journalists to come in and look at some of the internal communications at Twitter after he bought it, and this was published as the so-called "Twitter Files." That information was coming out in parallel with what we were discovering in the case and was confirming more or less what we were saying.

67. So we have multiple sources on the part of the companies themselves. Then, we have the internal documents that we got from the government discovery. We would like the court to make a ruling or endorse a reasonable settlement because the next administration could reverse an executive order with a new executive order. It would be good to have a ruling in Federal Court saying that the government can't do this. So that's the status of the case, which looks like it will establish a precedent that the government cannot coerce or unduly influence social media companies to censor constitutionally protected speech.

68. Laurie: *You've talked about free speech and the dignity of life, but you have also been involved in increasing awareness of other areas* *of ethical concern. What about hot topics such as Artificial Intelligence (AI) and its effect on life?*

69. Aaron: I gave a talk recently at Hillsdale College on AI and Transhumanism. AI is powerful, but, as I said during the Q&A of that talk, basically, we need to always treat AI as a tool and never elevate it to become an idol. I've had patients tell me, "Hey, I went to Chat GPT (or Grok, one of these large language models) and did a query, asking, 'What are the common side effects of this antidepressant medication that I'm considering taking because I want to learn more about it?'" Well, assuming the algorithm is good and drawing on reliable sources of information, that could be a good way to synthesize information presented in a summary in a way that a patient can easily understand. I'm fine with that augmenting my conversation with the patient about potential side effects of this medication. That worries me less than the patient - and I have had patients say this - who went to Chat GPT and said, "Given my medical history, should I take this antidepressant?"

70. Treating AI as a source of wisdom, discernment, judgment, or as a sort of oracle telling me how to make important decisions in my life and how to live - I think that's very dangerous. The whole concept of an idol, which you see running throughout the Bible, especially the Old Testament, is useful here. What is an idol? An idol is something we've created that is the work of our hands. That might be an interesting artifact, work of art, or useful tool, but instead of treating it as such, we elevate it to something above us and look to it for answers. If we put it in place of God or in place of other people or higher things, then it always comes back to bite us in the end.

71. Artificial intelligence is not actually intelligent. It's just a means. It's just a tool to synthesize information that human beings have already produced. I worry if we start treating it as a kind of oracle or a font of wisdom or an idol, it's going to come back to bite us. It's ultimately going to be certain human beings who have control over those algorithms exercising undue power control over others. So we can't treat this thing as though it's a god.

72. Laurie: *That's a very good summary; it encapsulates the concerns well.*

73. Aaron: Is AI a useful tool for certain things? Sure, I've used it to help synthesize research. It's great for pulling citations, too, like if I have a quote and I don't know what page number it's on. I can go to Grok and ask, "What page of Illich's *Medical Nemesis* is this quote found on?" It'll give you this. It's great. It's a great citation manager. So, it's very useful for certain things, such as summaries, citations, and stuff like that. Not, "How should I live my life?"

74. Laurie: *In speaking about the Dignity of Life, what about gene therapy, stem cell transfer, and In Vitro Fertilization (IVF)?*

75. Aaron: Oh, yes. I could go on and on with this stuff. Articles are where I really synthesize my thoughts. [See www.aaronkheriaty.com.] I recently wrote a piece on Preimplantation Genetic Testing (PGT), and In Vitro Gametogenesis (IVG) which are tied up with IVF. There's a danger now with IVF. IVF has so many problems associated with it. We have millions of embryos in cryopreservation - basically, cold storage. Saint John Paul II acknowledged [*Dignitas Personae*] that we've created a situation in which there is no perfectly just resolution. I know a lot of Christians are in favor of embryo adoption, which you can make an argument for. I think there are still problems ethically associated with embryo adoption that worry me. Maybe it's the best thing we can do under the circumstances, but there's no way we're going to find people to adopt millions of embryos. The alternative is to let these embryos die, which is also, obviously, not a just resolution.

76. It's just a terrible situation we've created, which was foreseeable, but nobody wanted to think about it. Parents using IVF don't want to, even if they're told, "You're going to have to make a decision for the disposition of the embryos that we do not implant in the future." They're so focused on having a baby that they don't think about it until later, and then they're sort of stuck, and they don't know what to do. They don't want to destroy their embryos because they know what they are. Now, it's like, "Yes, I have a child that's been born from this. I know that this is not just a clump of cells. I don't want to donate it to research. I don't want to adopt it out to another family because I don't necessarily want a genetically related child out there that's being raised by someone else. And so, I just avoid the issue." The Catholic Church tried to warn the world about IVF. Nobody listened. Now, we have a situation that's only growing worse by the

day of human life being frozen in this state of suspended animation and no way to resolve this issue.

77. There are all kinds of other problems associated with IVF that I don't have time to get into. But there's a danger now of using IVF combined with Preimplantation Genetic Testing (PGT) to have a new kind of consumer-driven eugenics. And then IVG, which is the creation of artificial gametes from skin cells, will multiply those problems thousandfold. Right now, we're limited in the number of embryos we can create by the difficulties of the egg harvesting procedure. Maybe you get half a dozen embryos from an IVF cycle, and it's invasive. It's intrusive. It's hard on the woman's body. It's bad enough that half of those get put in cold storage indefinitely. But with IVG, we could potentially create hundreds of embryos very easily by reprogramming skin cells to become sperm or eggs. That is being perfected in mice, and it's probably going to be feasible in humans sometime in the next ten years.

78. Laurie: *Oh no!*

79. Aaron: I wrote a little policy piece on that [*Preimplantation Genetic Testing and In Vitro Gametogenesis*], basically for busy staffers in Washington to understand the issue.[6] But yes, the problems associated with IVF are not going away; they're going to probably get worse in the next decade by the introduction of these ancillary technologies around IVF. That's going to take the problems that are already there and make them even worse, I anticipate.

80. I did a recent interview with Lila Rose, posted on my Substack [*Human Flourishing*]. [7] We covered a lot of different topics in that interview, including some of the stuff we've already talked about that happened during Covid and my free speech case, but I think the last thirty/thirty-five minutes of the interview get into IVG. That will give a good overview if you're interested in learning more.

---

[6] Available at https://eppc.org/wp-content/uploads/2025/03/3-Preimplantation-Genetic-Testing-and-In-Vitro-Gametogenesis.pdf

[7] Available at https://aaronkheriaty.substack.com/p/covid-shots-transhumanism-and-ai

81. I mean, it gets really weird. Two men having a baby, or two women having a baby that's genetically related to both of them, creating sperm from women and eggs from men. It's pretty dystopian.

82. Laurie: *Yes. And we probably don't even fully realize today all the problems it will create tomorrow.*

83. Aaron: No, we don't even have the intellectual resources to think through what it's going to do to our notions of lineage and family structure.

84. There are ethicists who are enthusiastic about this technology that talk about and are excited about so-called "Multiplex Parenting." Suppose you have four people of any sex who want to have a genetically related child. You take skin cells from one pair of the four, create sperm and eggs, and create an embryo in the lab. Then, do the same thing with the second pair of people and create an embryo in the lab. Extract embryonic stem cells from each of the embryos, reprogram them to become sperm and eggs, and create yet a third embryo, discarding the first two. Now, bring that third embryo to birth. Technically, those four people are the genetic grandparents of the child. But that's their quote, unquote "child." This is the so-called "Multiplex Parenting."

85. Theoretically, you could do that cycle multiple times once you start creating the embryos, extracting stem cells and creating gametes from those stem cells. You could do four or five generations and then bring someone to birth whose genetic parents, grandparents, great-grandparents, great-great-grandparents, whatever, were all embryos that were created and destroyed in a laboratory. Thus, compressing in space and time the generations, the person's lineage, and their genetic identity. We don't even have the intellectual resources to think through, "What is that?" And yet there are enthusiasts who think, "Yes, this is a great idea. Wouldn't it be awesome if eight people could all have a genetically related 'child'?"

86. Laurie: *It makes me think of how birth control [the pill and contraception] was thought to be freeing for women, but ultimately led to more disrespect and abuse. Right? And so we don't know how this focus on the benefits doesn't fully take into consideration the repercussions.*

87. Aaron: Exactly. Of course, this will be sold on the hard case that tugs on our hearts: the woman who had ovarian cancer and whose ovaries have been removed. She's married, has a loving husband, and wants to have a baby. Who wouldn't want to help them have a genetically related child? Since her ovaries are gone, we could just create eggs from her skin cells. That will be the wedge: the woman who had cancer saying, "Let's have a baby." Of course, who can argue with that, right? And then, before long, you're embracing "Multiplex Parenting," and God knows what else.

88. Here's another weird scenario. You're the maid working at the hotel where [a superstar actor] is staying. You decide you want to have his baby, but you fail to seduce him in the old-fashioned way to try to get pregnant, and he checks out of the hotel. Well, no worries! You could just go to his pillow and scrape some of his skin cells off his pillow and bring them to the rogue IVG Clinic - and you have [superstar actor's] babies! This is technically feasible, assuming this is perfected in humans. You start getting those kinds of scenarios. It's like, "Whoa! This is scary."

89. Laurie: *Well, what a note to leave this on. That is a scary thought! I think it shows the importance of teaching ethics to the next generation of medical professionals, as well as society as a whole - you've incorporated ethics, as well as medical topics, into teaching and publishing books, correct?*

90. Aaron: Yes. While I was at the University, I taught the required Ethics and Behavioral Science Course to the first and second-year medical students for several years. I was able to develop the ethics course kind of from scratch. That was more classroom-based teaching or small group seminar-style discussion in the preclinical years, which are the first two years of medical school. I also taught in the clinical years. I taught in the required psychiatry clerkship that all the third years have to rotate through for six weeks, and I taught fourth-year students who were doing a month-long elective in psychiatry.

91. Before I took over the Medical Ethics Program, I was the Residency Training Director in Psychiatry for five or six years. I oversaw the thirty-three residents in the program, which is a four-year program following medical school for specialty training in

psychiatry. So, I did a lot of clinical teaching, making bedside rounds with students and residents. I also did teaching as the Ethics Consult lead on the Ethics Committee, where we always had student members of the Ethics Committee.

92. So I had this third- and fourth-year hospital-based clinical teaching in the wards (which I very much enjoyed) and in the outpatient setting, supervising cases and doing psychotherapy supervision for senior residents in psychiatry. But I also had some classroom-based, lecture and seminar-based, more traditional teaching. I love teaching.

93. Teaching is the one thing I have not been able to reproduce to the same degree outside of the University. Everything else, including my research, clinical work, public policy work, and administrative roles, I've been able to do in private practice. I still do teaching; I still get lecture invitations and teaching invitations here and there, such as Hillsdale College. But the sort of regular clinical teaching that I was doing at the University, I'm not doing so much of anymore. I would say that's one thing I do miss a little bit, that day-to-day work with the medical students and residents. I come from a family of teachers, and it was very rewarding.

94. After my father became a deacon, he started teaching Catholic Catechism/Catholic religion classes in the parish school. My mother became a school counselor for many years. My sister was a teacher and then became a high school administrator. She married a teacher who also became a high school administrator. My brother is a chemistry science teacher at a school in St. Louis, and he married someone who has a tutoring program. So, our whole family has been involved in teaching and education. I guess it's sort of in the blood for me to have that interest in and love for teaching.

95. You also asked about the books. My first book, and my most commercially successful book, is called *The Catholic Guide to Depression*, through Sophia Institute Press. Their editor reached out to me several years ago and said, "We want to do a series on mental health but approach it from a Catholic perspective, combining the insights of modern psychiatry and modern psychology with the Catholic ascetical tradition. Do you know anyone who might be interested?" And I said, "Well, I could probably write a book like

that, and maybe you should start with depression because it's a very common affliction. I think that would be a good place to start." So, I wrote this book, and it's done well for a book that was written for a niche religious audience.

96. I've had edifying feedback from readers, [including] priests and pastors who tell me it's a helpful book to give people they're providing pastoral care to who may be struggling with depression or family members who have a loved one and they're trying to understand this illness and how to best support their loved one through it. That was a really great project.

97. I received a very beautiful voicemail from a reader in Canada a few years ago. She didn't leave a callback number, so I never actually spoke to her, but she said, "I was contemplating suicide, and I was in despair. Then I read your book, and it gave me hope. It helped me start that road to recovery." That's the kind of feedback that a writer wants to hear! I mean, [paraphrasing] "Your book saved my life." It's like, wow! It was worth writing just for that one person.

98. Laurie: *Exactly!*

99. Aaron: I also co-authored a book called *Transformative Conversations* with three other academics on a model we developed for peer mentoring groups in higher education. That was another early book that I did.

100. And then, after the University of California and I parted ways over the Covid vaccine mandate, I wrote a book on what happened to us during the pandemic and some of the government overreach that I thought society engaged in. It was a critique of our Covid policies but also a look at how some of these problems might continue to emerge in the future with declared states of emergency, with the overreach of public health agencies, and so forth. That book was called *The New Abnormal.*

101. I have another book that's currently in the pipeline, which will be published in September. That book is about medical education, and it's also a critique of contemporary medicine that's implicit in that. I wrote the first draft of the book twenty years ago when I finished medical school but never got it published. I sort of shopped

it around, but I didn't have a platform. I didn't have a name and wasn't able to gain any traction on it. The book is called *Making the Cut*. The subtitle is *How to Heal Modern Medicine*. It's about sixty percent narrative account of what I went through in medical school and what I learned during medical school, and about forty percent philosophical reflection on those experiences with an implicit critique of what I perceive has gone wrong in certain areas of contemporary healthcare systems, and what we might do to get that back on track. It's an interesting book because the narrative part was written a couple of decades ago, and the reflection on it was written last year. We'll see if all of that hangs together. We'll see what readers think of it. You never know until you publish something, but that book is coming out in September.

102. Then, I have another book that I'm pitching to publishers with my agent. That is an introduction to an Italian philosopher named Augusto Del Noce. He's not very well known in English. He's a Catholic philosopher who died in 1989 and wrote a lot about 19th-century philosophies and how they played out in 20th-century history. He grew up in Italy during the rise of Italian fascism, which caused him great concern. He wrote a lot about 20th-century totalitarian systems, Fascism, Nazism, Communism, and their roots in 19th-century Marxist and Hegelian philosophy. He also wrote about the technocratic scientism that emerged in the post-war years in the West. His writing is very relevant for not only understanding 20th-century history but also understanding our own contemporary history and what's happened in the West since the fall of Communism.

103. He died a couple of weeks after the fall of the Berlin Wall, and his last essay, which was written just before he died, was paradoxically entitled *Marxism Died in the East Because It Realized Itself in the West*. He wasn't talking about Marxist economics, which died with Communism. He was talking about the philosophical aspects of Marxist atheistic materialism.

104. I got exposed to his thoughts a few years ago. I got to know his English translator, Carlo Lancellotti, who's now translated three of his books into English. Del Noce is difficult to read if you don't have a background in Continental Philosophy. And so, I thought, "We need a little primer! We need a short, 150-175-page introduction that

would help English-speaking readers." He's an extraordinary thinker! He was almost prophetic, not because he could see into the future, but because he could discern the deep underlying philosophical tendencies that were animating the culture, the principles that were guiding historical developments. He could see where they were headed because he would follow them rigorously to their logical conclusions.

105. In the 1950s he predicted the fall of Soviet Communism under the weight of its own internal contradictions at a time when the rest of the world was thinking the Cold War and the Soviet Empire were going to be a permanent feature of foreseeable history. In 1970 he predicted the advent of gay marriage before anyone, even on the left, was talking about this as a serious proposal. He discerned the underlying principles of the sexual revolution of 1968 and saw exactly where this was going to take us. A remarkably prescient thinker that still has a lot to say to us.

106. Laurie: *That is going to be wonderful. There's so much to look forward to from the instruction side and from the philosophy side. Because we're talking about students and the challenges in the world today, please talk a little about what you see as challenges for people going into the medical profession in particular, and what we can do to help address those challenges.*

107. Aaron: Sure. A faithful Catholic going to medical school or navigating the medical profession can encounter challenges in terms of pressure to participate in procedures or to assist with procedures that would be contrary to the Catholic Faith and Morals. Sometimes opting out of assisting on an abortion or opting out of assisting on a procedure that would result intentionally in permanent sterilization, for example, could be difficult for a medical student who's at the bottom of the hospital hierarchy; sometimes subtle forms of retaliation can occur and pressure from the higher-ups that want you to just fall in line and conform - even though federal law does provide conscience protections for physicians and medical trainees. Likewise with the push now for the medicalizing of gender ideology.

108. So there are moral challenges for students, and students going into particular specialties, like obstetrics and gynecology, might face even greater challenges trying to get through residency training in a

28

way that is consistent with living Catholic Faith and Morals, which really is living sound Hippocratic medicine as well. But medicine has lost its way in the embrace of abortion, doctor-assisted suicide and euthanasia, and "gender reassignment" (or more accurately, sex rejecting) procedures that end up doing more harm than good. That's one challenge that many faithful medical students have to navigate.

109. I think there are other challenges in medicine. I've written a series of articles recently about managerialism in medicine; these themes will emerge in my next book, too. Managerialism is an ideology of top-down rigid control that attempts to impose uniformity on the practice of medicine and control it from above. Many physicians working in large healthcare institutions are dealing with programs like Medicare that exercise enormous control over the practice of medicine. They experience a sense that the rigid system within which they're working does not permit them to offer the kind of medical care that their patients need.

110. There's this concept in ethics called moral distress, which is developed to explain a lot of physician burnout. Physicians are not burning out today in large part because they work long hours or their work is difficult. That may be true, but there are a lot of studies that suggest that the real reason for physician burnout is not long hours or arduous work but working within a system where they feel they have to compromise good patient care for the sake of surviving within that system.

111. And many patients feel this; they go to the hospital, or they go to a clinic that's run by a large healthcare organization, and it's sort of the experience of going to Disneyland, where you're in what I call turnstile medicine. You're sort of shuffled through the system: you wait in the lines, you go through this turnstile, you get the same thing from every person that you see, and the care is not tailored to your individual needs. The doctor spends more time staring at a computer screen than he does looking you in the eye, face-to-face or examining you. He's asking a series of questions that are built into the electronic medical record so he can check a bunch of boxes that have nothing to do with your chief complaint, nothing to do with the ailment that you're seeking treatment for.

112. Patients don't like the system, physicians don't like the system, and the system is becoming unsustainable economically as well. These are difficult problems. I don't claim to have all the solutions to them, but whatever the solutions are, they need to be moving toward a more decentralized method of healthcare delivery, where we can allow new models to flourish and new experiments in healthcare financing and healthcare delivery to be tried, some of which will pan out and some of which won't.

113. I think if the tendency to increasingly centralized control that we've seen over the last several decades continues, we're going to see fewer good people interested in going into medicine and practicing. In that context, we're going to continue to get suboptimal health outcomes. We're spending more money on healthcare in the United States than any other country in the world, and we're not even breaking the top forty in terms of health outcomes when it comes to developed countries. Something is wrong with our healthcare system.

114. The chronic disease epidemic can't be laid entirely at the feet of medicine. There are other contributing factors that have become part of the public conversation recently. What's going on with our food? What's going on with our farming? But certainly, there are necessary reforms in medicine that we need to make in order to bring medicine back to a traditional Hippocratic approach, where the doctor-patient relationship is at the center of the healing enterprise.

115. So I wouldn't dissuade students from going into medicine. Certainly, those who have the talent should pursue it. We need good and faithful people to become doctors, but it's important to go in with eyes wide open and to understand what some of the current challenges are within the healthcare system.

116. **Laurie:** *I know there's a National Catholic Bioethics Center [ncbcenter.org], and you're writing books. What other kinds of resources are there for them?*

117. **Aaron:** Certainly, if you need an ethics consultation, the National Catholic Bioethics Center is a great resource. The Catholic Medical Association [cathmed.com] has chapters around the country, opportunities for student mentorship, and a very good conference every year where students can meet other Catholic physicians.

118. Along with doctors from Harvard, Stanford, and Duke University, I recently founded something called the Hippocratic Society [hippsoc.org], which is not confessionally Christian. It's not specifically religious, but it's an attempt to have a medical society that is dedicated to the proposition that medicine should be aimed always, and only, at healing. Things that are contrary to healing - reshaping the human body, euthanizing someone at their request, killing an unborn child - these things don't have a rightful place in medicine. The Hippocratic Society also is primarily directed toward students and residents. We have pre-med chapters now at a couple of universities, and we have med student and resident-focused chapters at several medical schools. It's only a couple of years old, but it is growing; we have new chapters springing up in various places. We have a new podcast that we just launched. So I would say that the Hippocratic Society is another resource that would be very helpful hopefully for students or pre-meds that are considering pursuing a career in medicine.

119. Laurie: *Excellent! As I listen to you, I'm thinking of the aspect of the natural moral law. Science is synergistic; it's not contrarian to the Catholic Faith.*

120. Aaron: That's exactly right. I think that [the natural moral law] is at the heart of what the Hippocratic Society is trying to do. As a result, it's probably going to be attractive to many people of faith, Catholic, Protestant, Jewish, Muslim, and so forth; those folks wouldn't surprise me if they were disproportionately represented among our membership. But also, everything that we're doing is simply consistent with the good practice of medicine. One doesn't need to be a person of faith in order to recognize that.

Faith

Leadership

Life

Part 2
Faith

*What I learned from St. Jerome is that a failure offered to God is
more valuable than a success not offered to God.*
(para. 136)

*Learn that little prayer. "Doce me passionem Tuam" (Teach me your
suffering), and try to redirect your focus on the crucified Christ
rather than on our own troubles.*
(para. 210)

121. Laurie: *We are shifting gears a little to talk about having a
strong foundation to build upon - your faith. What's your earliest
religious experience or memory?*

122. Aaron: Well, I certainly have fond memories. It's not my earliest
memory, but I have a very fond memory of my First Communion and
my first Confession; those childhood sacraments of initiation. (I was
an infant, so I don't remember my baptism!)

123. As more of a private devotion/personal piety, I do recall my
Mom, during Lent, would often bring us to the parish when no one
else was there. The lights were sort of dim, and we would walk into
the parish, making the Stations of the Cross. That early exposure to a
slower and more deliberate kind of meditation on our Lord's passion
made a deep impression on me. I remember fondly, as a child, the
experience of being at our parish, alone with our Lord there in the
tabernacle, and just me, my mom, my brother, and my sister praying
together was very powerful.

124. So that was a memory from my early childhood that sticks with
me of how my mother not only brought us to Mass, brought us to
Confession and sent us to Catholic school, but also shared that kind
of personal piety, using that traditional devotion of the Stations of the
Cross. It was very formative for me in my own prayer. So, my wife

and I have tried to pray together with our own children - like praying the family Rosary together. If we're out and about, you know, like driving my kids to soccer practice - well, let's stop on the way home at the local church or the local chapel at the Catholic High School and make a visit to the Blessed Sacrament. Let's just go in for a few minutes and say hello to our Lord.

125. I don't have parenting advice. Anyone who claims to be an expert on parenting, I think, automatically disqualifies themselves as such. I'm certainly no expert. Every child is different. You just have to pray, pray, pray, but if I could give any advice, it would be to pray also with your children and let your children see you pray. Let them see that! Mom or dad is someone who sits down at home and reads scripture or sits down at home and prays, who prays with us at times and teaches us how to pray. I think that is the best thing that you could do for your children. They need catechesis. Obviously, they need intellectual formation, but they also need to learn how to become men and women of prayer.

126. That's where parents and grandparents can have such a powerful role by setting an example, and also inviting their children to pray: Teach them the Rosary, or how to make the Stations of the Cross and other traditional prayers of the [Catholic] Church, whether it's the Liturgy of the Hours or the Divine Mercy Chaplet. Every family is different. They have their own private devotions, all of which are wonderful. But for us, trying to cultivate Eucharistic piety, a devotion to Our Lady in the Rosary, and praying the Angelus at noon has been part of our family culture.

127. Laurie: *You mentioned earlier that life is not always easy. You were blessed with a very wonderful childhood. Not everyone has that. But even in your own life, you mentioned some challenges. Can you talk about how your faith has helped you through them?*

128. Aaron: I suffered from a chronic pain condition for almost five years that was nearly disabling. It resulted from a ruptured disc in my spine and two failed spine surgeries. I had nerve pain going down my left leg from that spinal injury, and it was only relieved by lying down. Pain medications, even heavy pain medications, would take the edge off temporarily - I spent the better part of four years lying down!

129. Laurie: *Was this when you had children?*

130. Aaron: Yes, this is from about 2016 to 2020. I had five children still at home, which was challenging, obviously, and put a tremendous burden on my wife because there was less that I could do physically.

131. In any other medical specialty, I would have been disabled. If I had to be sitting or standing on my feet as a surgeon, I would not have been able to function. As a psychiatrist, I developed a novel method of therapy where I would lie down on the couch, and the patient would sit in the chair. It was sort of a reverse Freudian method! My patients all got used to it. I had a zero-gravity chair that would basically make me horizontal. I was able to barely get by and continue working during that time, but that was a heavy cross to carry. It was humbling and sometimes humiliating. I spent a lot of time in church, lying down in the back on a bench, which I'm sure looked odd and strange to many of the parishioners who didn't know why I was doing that.

132. So I have been given certain challenges in life. When I lost my job at the University of California Irvine, that was a challenge. Basically, I came to the point where I said, "I can't, in good conscience, support this vaccine mandate policy. I believe in the principle of informed consent. I'm willing to sacrifice my career on the basis of that principle." So, I tried to challenge that policy in Federal Court. If you want to go sideways quickly with your employer, a good way to do that is to sue them in Federal Court!

133. They very quickly retaliated by firing me, and I didn't really have a parachute or a Plan B. I had to scramble to put together a private practice and figure out how I was going to continue to do my other work. Fortunately, God took care of us, and it all worked out. But, that first year after I was fired was challenging because I was still the primary breadwinner for a family of five children.

134. If you want to ask, "What did I learn from that?" Well, I learned from St. Josemaría Escrivá that we need to offer all of our work to God. We need to try to do it as well as humanly possible. We want to give him [God] the best of what we're capable of doing and try to do it with as much perfection as we're capable of, without

becoming neurotically perfectionistic, which is not the idea; give him the best of what we have, but also, in humility, recognize that we're not, at least from a human point of view, always going to be successful. We have to offer to God everything, which means we have to offer to God not only our successes (like our Saint Juan Diego Leadership for the World Award from TLI and the plaudits) but we have to offer him our "failures" as well.

135. Saint Jerome, who I've learned more about in recent years, was obviously a brilliant theologian. He translated the Bible from Hebrew and Greek into Latin - the Latin Vulgate Bible of the Church. The first edition was done by St. Jerome, and he had a very strong, kind of choleric personality. He didn't suffer fools gladly. He was stubborn; the saints are not perfect. He probably struggled with pride because he was both brilliant and extremely choleric. He didn't want to translate the so-called Apocrypha, the books of the Old Testament originally written in Greek, but the Council of Rome and the Church said, "No, these are part of the Canon of Scriptures, and you need to translate those as well." He kind of pitched a fit publicly, but he did it. He ended up swallowing his pride, and he did it.

136. He [St. Jerome] realized that everything good that we have to offer to God is actually first his [God's] gift to us; the only thing of our very own, that's really mine, that I have to offer to God is my sins, when you stop and think about it. So that's humbling, and it should be. The only thing I have to offer to God is my nothingness. But he actually wants me to offer that to him, too, maybe most of all. What I learned from St. Jerome is that a failure offered to God is more valuable than a success not offered to God.

137. So yes, we try to do our best. Yes, we try to do our work humanly well. We want to give Jesus the first fruits. We want to give Jesus the unblemished lamb, the choicest animal of the flock. God was very clear with Old Testament sacrifices that he wanted the best of what the Jewish people had to offer, not their old mangy lamb that was on its last leg. He didn't want our leftovers. He doesn't want our half-hearted efforts, but he still wants everything from us. And you know, he still loves us even when we lose our jobs, even when we try something and fail, even when we publish a book and nobody buys it.

138. Those things may be, from the supernatural point of view, especially good for us because they're helpful in growing in humility. They're helpful for recognizing our nothingness. They're helpful for, at the end of the day, recognizing that the only thing that's truly mine that I have to offer to God is my sins. Everything else good that I have to offer him was first his gift to me, anyway, either his natural gifts, the talents that he gave me, or a gift of his Grace to accomplish this with his supernatural help.

139. So that's a lesson that I've been trying to learn. Maybe my chronic pain condition helped me begin to learn that lesson. Maybe losing my job at the University was another opportunity for me to learn that lesson. Of course, we want to be successful, humanly speaking, but I think leadership is not primarily about success. It's about our intention to serve God in everything and our willingness to offer him everything, including our nothingness, and our inability, and our "failures."

140. Laurie: *Recognizing that it's actually healthy when you encounter challenges is such a powerful lesson, but also a benefit from a mental health standpoint, right?*

141. Aaron: That's right, and God doesn't love me any less because my movie script didn't get picked up or my book flopped. St. Josemaría Escrivá has a point in one of his homilies where he says, "A Christian is not a neurotic collector of good behavior reports." (Christ is Passing By, Number 75.) That is a really helpful phrase. Christian perfection is not the same as human perfectionism. Obviously, God wants a soldier to be brave in battle, but he loves that soldier just as much if that soldier cowers in fear and wants to wave the white flag, or God loves him more because that person recognizes in that moment of humiliation that he needs God more and that he's in need of God's Grace and power and salvation.

142. So I think, yes, from a mental health perspective, it's really important for us to get away from the notion that we somehow need to earn God's love by being good. Yes, God wants us to grow in the virtues. Yes, God wants to, with his Grace, help us to grow in holiness, of course. But he doesn't love us any less when we fall short, and when we struggle, and still fail to achieve that kind of perfection.

143. Laurie: *Along with that perfectionism perspective, some people think the Catholic Faith is like a rigid set of rules. How would you respond to a person who feels that way?*

144. Aaron: I would say that at the center of the Catholic Faith is the Cross of Jesus Christ; that is the manifestation of his love, and that is something that he did and would do again for each of us, alone and individually. And he did it even for the people who reject him.

145. So the first thing I would say is that the Catholic Faith is not at its center a list of rules and regulations. At the center of the Catholic Faith is the blood and water that flowed from Jesus's pierced side, his Cross and his passion which actually began at the Incarnation. It's his humility to divest himself of his divine glory and become an embryo in the womb of Our Lady and live an ordinary life as a craftsman in Nazareth, and his suffering for our sake, culminating obviously in his arrest on Holy Thursday, his agony in the Garden of Gethsemane, his passion and death on Good Friday, and his being dead on Holy Saturday. That's the central mystery of the Catholic Faith, which led to, of course, his glorious resurrection!

146. And because God loves us, he does give us warning signs. That's what the Ten Commandments are, and that's what our Lord's teachings are - Look, if you live this way, it will lead you to misery. A good parent corrects and even chastises their little child who runs into traffic, not because they want to make the child feel bad or guilt trip them but precisely because they love the child and they don't want the child to be hurt or harmed. That's what a loving father does.

147. So while the rules are not at the center, the rules are also not trivial. But the rules make sense when we first contemplate our Lord's suffering and that he loved us first - not because we deserved it, not because we can do anything to earn it, but simply because that's who he is.

148. I would just say you may not have very much to offer to God, but offer him the little that you have and then see what he does with it. Give him your five loaves and your two fish, even if it doesn't look very impressive. Have faith that he can multiply it. And if you think you have more than five loaves and two fish to give him, you're mistaken. You actually don't. All you have came from him.

149. Laurie: *Earlier you mentioned taking your children to a church on the way home from soccer practice. People often mention to me that they struggle fitting faith and prayer into their busy family and professional life. I've shared with them the use of visual triggers to encourage more regular and spontaneous prayers, such as prayer cards on my desk, a Rosary on my rearview mirror, icons or a crucifix where I can see them when I lift my head up from the computer, even encapsulating fragments of scripture into passwords. So, I'm curious. Do you use any visual triggers, or do you have any other tips for more effective incorporation of faith to improve daily life?*

150. Aaron: I do. [Reaching into his pocket, Aaron pulls out a small metal crucifix and kisses it.] I carry a small pocket crucifix that I like to kiss and place on my desk. It's subtle. It's not, you know, in your face for people who come here to see me in my office who may not be sharing the same faith. I don't have a gigantic crucifix or picture of the crucified Christ on my wall. That might be intimidating to patients. But [pointing the crucifix] it's there, and they can notice it if they want to.

151. It [the crucifix] is a good reminder when I'm doing my work and trying to offer my work up to God, and I'm getting tired, or want to cut corners, or, you know, go surf social media rather than attend to the task at hand. I glance down at the crucifix, and I offer a little aspiration or a little prayer for the person I'm praying for and offering my work for, and then I try to get back to work. So yes, those little visual reminders can be helpful, and they could be subtle. They could just be a couple of paper clips in the shape of a cross that I put down on my desk.

152. The excuse you always hear in regard to prayer is, "I don't have time, and my life is really busy." But my response to that is people make time, they protect time, for the things that are really important. Honestly, if you don't make time for prayer, it's simply because you don't want to pray. If you really want to pray, like, if you really want to get in shape, you'll make time to go to the gym - if you really want it - not just wistfully, "Oh, wouldn't it be nice if I was more fit" (Or, nice if I dropped a few pounds, or if I could run a 10K.) No, if you really want it, you'll put on the running shoes, and you'll go do it. That's the same with prayer. If you really want it, you'll make time for

it, and you have time. How much time are you spending watching TV? How much time are you spending on social media? How much time are you spending reading the news? Do you need to read twelve articles about what happened yesterday that's soon to be forgotten, or can you read one or two and then spend the other twenty minutes saying the Rosary or doing some mental prayer?

153. Laurie: *Speaking of the things that are in the news, there's the sex abuse scandal within the Church. It's an ongoing topic of news and discussion, kind of an open wound. What role do you think we have as laity to help with that healing?*

154. Aaron: I think we, the laity, need to insist on transparency and accountability from the bishops. My own view on this is not sanguine. I don't think we have actually learned anything, or we don't seem in many cases to have learned anything from the sex abuse crisis. What we've put in place, [such as] safe environment trainings are not going to prevent a pedophile from harming a child. A pedophile can run through an online safe environment training and answer all the questions correctly and still go and harm and abuse children. I don't think those things are actually useful at all. I think they're window-dressing.

155. I think the institutional practices and mentality that facilitated the problem in the first place, basically, have continued. I haven't seen any changes in that regard, and by that, I mean protecting the institution at all costs: Don't admit when you were wrong, don't investigate problems, and consult lawyers whose job it is to engage in risk management.

156. Laurie: *It almost sounds like going to Confession without being truly repentant.*

157. Aaron: Yes, I think the bishops are so afraid now of liability because we've spent so much money on payouts that what they seem to have learned is, "I need to protect the Church from liability; whenever I make a decision on anything, I need to consult lawyers whose job it is to make sure we don't get sued or taken to court or prosecuted in some way." That's not a good way to make decisions, especially in a culture that is hostile to your values and your aims. But still, it seems to me that risk management lawyers are sort of running the show. It may, incidentally, in certain circumstances, help to protect children, but it's not the main thing that we need to do. The main thing that we need to do to help protect children is transparency and accountability.

158. [For example], if you practice medicine according to the principle of "just don't get sued," you won't practice good medicine. Actually, you'll practice defensive medicine. You won't intervene on hard cases where you don't have a guaranteed outcome. So, the sickest people don't get treatment. You'll order excessive and unnecessary tests to try to, we call it "CYA (cover your butt) Medicine." Obviously, you take reasonable measures to avoid malpractice lawsuits. But when that becomes your overriding concern, you're not actually practicing good medicine.

159. When your overriding concern is just to give the patient the best care possible, you are incidentally reducing your professional liability by doing that. It's a different framework; it's a different mentality. And I think the institutional Church needs to be about proclaiming the Gospel and pursuing holiness, and incidentally, that should reduce the instances of clerical sexual abuse. But, when the overriding concern just becomes don't get sued, the Church is not being the Church. I still see a lot of that from the bishops.

160. **Laurie:** *So, being sued is one of the potential threats to the Church, but what do you see as potential threats to the Catholic Faith? Are there problematic ideologies?*

161. **Aaron:** Oh, yes. Where do I begin? I would say we live in a culture that prioritizes well-being over all other values: well-being as understood in purely worldly, material, comfort-seeking ways - that the human person is sort of a bundle of material instincts and needs - and the purpose of life is to gratify those without getting thrown in jail. That is sort of the prevailing mentality - just optimizing my comforts and optimizing my material satisfaction seems to be the pervasive ethos of the culture.

162. Certainly, Catholics are not immune from those influences or from being affected by that mentality and by a kind of technological, instrumental rationality that sees everything else, including other human beings, as a means toward one's own selfish ends. So a society

where people are using one another, kind of instrumentally, all the time, rather than loving one another - I think that's a very serious danger. There's a danger of seeing the human person, and the human body especially, as sort of raw material to be manipulated. You see this in gender ideology and you see this in transhumanism - "I am just an autonomous will that's trapped inside this body that is basically just raw material for me to do whatever I want with."

163. Laurie: *How do you take St. John Paul II's Theology of the Body and bring it into personal life, like into marriage or into personal relationships? How do we look at the culture from a laity perspective through that lens?*

164. Aaron: Well, the antidote to this is, I think, living the sacramental principle. It's not just about having the right ideas; I mean, we need to combat these ideologies through a better philosophy, a better theology of the human person, a better anthropology, but also it is cultivated through Catholic practices, and especially through the sacraments.

165. The sacrament of marriage reminds us that the body is sacred. It is for the spouse and to be given in that way. You can't understand the Theology of the Body if you're not trying to actually live the theology of marriage - whether you're married or single - trying to live in a way that respects the body and that understands what human sexuality is for.

166. In participating in the sacraments and participating in Catholic worship, we're reminded that material things are part of God's creation and they've also been sanctified by the Incarnation of Christ. Christ took these ordinary material things and made them into means of Grace. So I think just living a Catholic sacramental life is an antidote to a culture that's becoming increasingly wedded to a disembodied, virtual, digital, abstract realm.

167. I think that churches should not have closed during the pandemic because that communicated to the Catholic faithful that watching Mass live streamed on TV is more or less the same as going to church - "I can do that; I can make a Spiritual Communion." Spiritual Communions are obviously good, but for many people this ended up meaning, "I don't really need to go to church." You saw that

many people didn't come back to church after the churches opened up again because churches had basically communicated to them, "It's actually not that important that you are here, and bare biological life should take precedence over your spiritual health."

168. The practice of going to Mass and receiving Communion and the practice of going to Confession face-to-face should be maintained. The Church has always maintained that Confession cannot be done over the phone. It cannot be done over Zoom; maybe in the future, that will change, I don't know. But that face-to-face presence of the priest and the penitent is a reminder of the fact that we exist in the created order as bodily beings that require sight, touch, taste, sound, and smell in order to engage even the highest spiritual things.

169. Saint Teresa of Avila says that in prayer, we can never get past the humanity of Christ and go right into some purely abstract spiritual realm of contemplation. We always have to come back to the humanity of Christ, His physical body, meditating on the actual wounds of the passion. It's not a higher spirituality to think that I can go beyond that into the purely spiritual realm where the humanity of Christ is sort of left behind and is something lower.

170. So, I think the antidote is living a Catholic sacramental life - a Catholic liturgical life. You know, where the smells and the bells, and the incense, and the stained glass, and all this stuff brings us back to the importance of the body in the created order.

171. **Laurie:** *That's why all the sacraments have both, the visible as a sign of the invisible grace, right?*

172. **Aaron:** That's right. The Word became flesh. The Word didn't become just an idea.

173. **Laurie:** *So what about finding hope? We've talked a lot about scandals and challenges, but there is also a great reason for hope. Can you touch on that?*

174. **Aaron:** Absolutely. We have to hope because we know the end of the story. We know that Christ has already triumphed over sin and death and human misery. Our hope is found in the Cross. [Some say],

"I can't hope because I'm suffering." No, your hope is found in the Cross. Does that mean every human thing will work out according to what I want? Does that mean that bad things won't happen? No, but it means that in the Cross - actually, on the Cross with him - we find Christ. There's no Easter Sunday without Good Friday. So, suffering and the Cross and difficulties in the Church and in the world do not rob us of our hope. They remind us that this is actually where our hope lies.

175. There's a prosperity gospel that infects not just Protestant Churches, but the Catholic Church to some extent as well. I think it's very prevalent in the United States. "If you believe, God will bless you with material abundance, and good things will happen to you. He'll cure your wife's cancer miraculously, and your business ventures are going to all work out." Well, it's true that God will bless you, including giving you various material blessings at times, but he will also bless you with the Cross. He gives the Cross to his friends. If you look at the lives of the saints, they tend to suffer actually more than people who lack their level of holiness because that draws them closer to Christ and his passion. That allows them to participate in his redemptive work. Bad things happening should not rob us of our hope. They should draw us closer to Christ on the Cross which is actually where our hope is found.

176. Laurie: *But it also doesn't mean that if there's suffering or pain, there is no joy, right? It's not that you're sentenced to a life of just suffering without any joy. Can you talk about joy in the midst of suffering?*

177. Aaron: Yes, St. Josemaría Escrivá had this very striking phrase where he described Christian joy as rooted in the shape of a cross. These two things are compatible. Again, if you look at the lives of the saints, you see this interior peace and this tranquility, even in the midst of their suffering. I wrote about Blessed Franz Jagerstatter [see Appendix] and that line in the film that I just love, "But I already am free." There's something in me that even this torture cannot take away. Saint Maximilian Kolbe was starved to death in Auschwitz, singing hymns of praise to God and leading others who were being killed to praise God in that way. It's not that these martyrs were necessarily braver than the rest of us. It's that they were madly in love with Jesus Christ. So, they had this interior joy, interior freedom, and interior peace that absolutely nothing could take from them. It was paradoxically even deepened through their suffering. They weren't robbed of that.

178. And of course, all of this should go without saying, but I'll mention it: all of this is compatible with trying to alleviate the suffering that we see in the world, too. Okay, it's the Cross. Do we have a kind of passive resignation in the face of human suffering? No, we try to relieve the misery of poverty and sickness. I'm a physician. So my job is to help reduce people's suffering! But I also recognize that suffering can never be completely eradicated in this fallen world. That fact, again, shouldn't rob us of our hope. It should draw us closer to the suffering Christ where we find joy and hope, ultimately the resurrection. These sufferings are nothing compared to the prize that awaits us in heaven, as Saint Paul put it.

179. Laurie: *You mentioned a couple of movies. Please talk a little bit about other movies or music that you have found particularly inspiring.*

180. Aaron: Sure. Music. I recently heard a live performance of Morten Lauridsen's *O Magnum Mysterium,* a beautiful vocal piece about the Eucharist. It's a beautiful contemporary piece. He [Lauridsen] is still alive. He's a retired professor of music at USC [University of Southern California]. I also love Bach and Mozart.

181. Then there are some contemporary bands that I like. Mumford and Sons is one of my favorites. There's something spiritually uplifting about their music. There is joy, but their songs are not "happy-clappy."' The older brother, James, of their lead singer, Marcus Mumford, is a good friend of mine. So, I'm fond of that contemporary band. And there's a lot of contemporary rock music I listen to with my kids. I was just listening to Bob Dylan this morning!

182. Music is wonderful. My wife is a musician. Several of my kids are musically talented. I am not very musically talented, but I do have a lot of appreciation for good music - classical music and some contemporary rock bands.

183. Movies. Yes, I'm a movie buff. I love good movies. My kids like to joke that I will watch a movie and try to find the spiritual meaning in

it and lecture them on it. My wife and I taught confirmation for several years, and we would have a movie night sometimes for the Confirmation kids.

184. *The Shawshank Redemption* is one of my favorite films. Bob Gunton [who plays] the prison warden, is a parishioner at my church. He's a great actor and villain in that movie. The main character in that movie, [Andy Dufresne (Tim Robbins)], is a Christ figure. He's unjustly condemned to prison, and then he has to crawl through, literally crawl through, shit in the sewer to emerge in his new life ~ an image of the death and resurrection of an innocent man. So that's a beautiful film.

185. Alfonso Cuaron's movie, *Gravity*, we've used with the confirmation kids. I can run through a whole exegesis of that movie. I don't know if you've seen that film?

186. Laurie: *Yes, but it's been a while.*

187. Aaron: I'll give you the five-minute version of my interpretation of that film. So, in the film, the heavens are the earth and the earth is heaven. They start out in outer space, which is symbolically this world, and they're trying to get back to earth, which is their home, which symbolically is heaven.

188. So they're out in outer space, and it opens with a tranquil scene of them tinkering with this space station. There are three astronauts. They hear over the radio news of a disaster at a distance. Some meteor has struck another satellite or something, and there is this shrapnel that's heading toward them. So that's The Fall; that's original sin introduced into the world. It comes around and it hits them; it destroys their ship and destroys their method of getting home.

189. It kills one of the three astronauts, and there's this image of death where you see his space helmet with a huge hole right in the middle of the face. It's a very striking image of death entering into this tranquil scene. Then you have this man and woman who need to figure out how to get home.

190. There's sort of this Adam and Eve, creation and fall. Adam and Eve are now struggling with this. The shrapnel, as it hits things,

creates more shrapnel, like a chain reaction. There's sort of the effects of sin multiplying. And it's going to come around. It's going to hit them again. It's going to be bigger this time.

191. Anyway, the story goes on, and they're struggling to figure out how to get to this other ship that might be able to bring them home. At one point, George Clooney, the male character, has to basically sacrifice his life to save the life of the female. They're tethered together. Unless he untethers himself, they're both going to float off into space and die. So, he does that and saves her, but he's gone.

192. At one point, there's this very interesting scene where she basically says, "No one ever taught me how to pray, and I don't really know how to pray." This is a scene where she is losing oxygen, and she passes out. She has a vision of him. She thinks - Oh, no, he's still alive; he's here. He tells her what to do to fix the problem, and then she wakes up and realizes, I just had a vision of him, or I had a dream of him or delirious delusion of him. So you have this sort of communion of the saints, intercession moment, where he helps her even after he has died.

193. Anyway, she finally gets to the ship that's capable of bringing her back home. She comes down to earth. She's burning up on reentry, crashes into a pond, and sinks to the bottom. She's got this heavy spacesuit on. She's undergoing this kind of baptism, which is a baptism into Christ's death. She's going to drown if she doesn't get this spacesuit off. So, that's taking off the old self and discarding the sin that's pulling her down and killing her.

194. Then, in the final scene of the film, she's stripped down to her underwear; She's sort of naked coming out of the waters of baptism. The last scene of the film is her stepping on solid ground. She's finally home. You see her foot stepping on the earth; she's made it. Then it pans up to the sky, and you see the shrapnel of her spaceship coming down; it is tongues of fire, and it's flaming. So, you have creation, fall, prayer, communion of the saints, Baptism, and Confirmation.

195. Laurie: *Pentecost - with the fire.*

196. Aaron: Pentecost, yes. So, I just think it's a great movie. Anyway, I love movies and I like trying to find spiritual meaning in movies. This sort of Bishop Barron approach.

197. Laurie: *Wow! I would have never viewed that movie that way.*

198. Aaron: Watch it again with that in mind! Use that as an interpretive lens. You'll probably spot other things. I mean, there's just a lot in that film. It's great!

199. Laurie: *Yes, it's a mindset of how you look at things. I used to use Princess Bride with the kids for dating and marriage discussions.*

200. Aaron: Last night, I watched *Friday Night Lights* with my kids, which is a football movie. It's a very interesting sports movie because most sports movies are about overcoming the odds and winning against the odds. *Friday Night Lights* is about losing. So, I had a little conversation with my kids about that after the film.

201. There are some really interesting lines in the film. At one point the coach tells the quarterback, "It took me a long time to realize that, uh, there ain't much difference between winnin' and losin' except for how the outside world treats you." The movie is about a high school football team in a small town in Texas that's totally football-obsessed. The whole town revolves around the high school football team. All the older guys in the town are trying to relive their glory days of playing football in high school and putting all this pressure on these kids to win.

202. It's a really well-done film. They end up going to the State Championship, but they don't win. They win a lot of games; it's a successful season. They get second in the state. But all the games they show in detail in the film are games they lost. And so, it's about losing. One of the main characters gets injured. He has this glorious football career ahead of him, and he gets injured. There's this heartbreaking scene where the uncle who's raising him is sitting in the car with him, and the player says, [paraphrasing] "I don't know what I am going to do now. All I know how to do is play football, and I can't play football. What am I going to do with this, my life?"

203. I really like that movie because you need to learn how to lose too, and not have it destroy you.

204. Laurie: *Find a lesson in it, right?*

205. Aaron: Yes I think the lesson of that film, the point is, to get out there and give everything you have. The score at the end doesn't matter as much as whether you actually love your teammates and can look them in the eye and tell them, "I gave it everything I had."

206. Laurie: *What recommendations would you have for a person to strengthen and practice their faith in light of all these challenges that exist? We talked about the medical profession's challenges, but what about even in other professions?*

207. Aaron: As a psychiatrist, I dive into people's suffering every day and probably have a unique window into the anguish of the human heart that many people don't have outside of their own personal experience with suffering. Our tendency, quite understandably, is to focus on our own suffering and to ask God, "Why? Why me?" "Why did I lose my job?" "Why is my spouse diagnosed with cancer, and why haven't you healed her yet? I've been praying for a miracle." "Why is my son (or daughter) struggling with this serious problem at school?" Or, "Why is there evil in the world, period?" I took an entire course on the problem of evil from a brilliant Christian philosopher at Notre Dame. You could spend a lifetime studying this philosophical question, "Why would an all-powerful, all-good, all-knowing God permit evil in the world?" It's natural to ask those questions, and Christian theologians and philosophers throughout the ages have struggled with that question. Many atheists become atheists, at least they claim, because they can't answer that question.

208. So, all that's understandable, but my advice would be to shift your focus from your own suffering to our Lord's suffering. I have a friend who taught me a little prayer, which has been very helpful to me and many of my patients. In Latin, it is *"Doce me passionem Tuam"* (Teach me your suffering). That short little aspiration, that short little prayer, shifts our focus from our own suffering to our Lord's. If we focus on, "How do I go deeper into and meditate more deeply upon our Lord's suffering?" That is what helps liberate us from our own; that's what helps us carry the Cross, which is his

50

Cross, which should be his Cross in our lives, and to see that we're not alone when we suffer.

209. We want to run from suffering. We want to avoid it. But it's sort of paradoxical to say, "Okay, in my own suffering, I'm going to actually try to attend more deeply to Christ's suffering, to contemplate his wounds, to remain with him in the garden and try to stay awake." The mystery of the Cross, the mystery of our Faith, somehow, by God's Grace, can help transform our suffering into something that is sanctifying. It doesn't necessarily mean that God will take away our suffering. It doesn't mean that it's going to magically disappear, but we can find a kind of deeper spiritual peace and consolation, even if, at the surface, we're still moaning and complaining. All of that is fine, and our Lord understands. I mean, our Lord Himself asked in the garden of Gethsemane to "Take this cup away from me," [Mathew 14:36] but he added, "Thy will be done." So, to recoil from suffering is perfectly natural and normal and human. That was part of even Jesus's own experience as he approached his passion. But then, to enter into his suffering, I think, is precisely what helps us carry our cross in a way.

210. So, that would be my advice. Learn that little prayer. *"Doce me passionem Tuam"* (Teach me your suffering), and try to redirect your focus on the crucified Christ rather than on our own troubles.

"DOCE ME PASSIONEM TUAM"

(Teach me your suffering)

"While I was praying to reconcile my suffering with His, to give it value by uniting it with His, Jesus gave me something immeasurably more valuable: He gradually taught me that I don't need to comprehend my own suffering. Whatever I have suffered or not in this life is of little consequence for finding true peace. The path to lasting peace, to genuine freedom, is in learning His suffering and embracing His Cross. For, like John the Baptist said, "He must increase but I must decrease" (John 3:30). I must eventually become nothing if I want to one day be united to the One I love." (CatholicExchange, Kheriaty, March 7, 2025)

Artwork: *The Crucifixion,* c. 1320/1325 **Bernardo Daddi**
Courtesy National Gallery of Art, Washington

Part 3

Leadership

There's this paradoxical aspect of the Catholic Faith that our Lord chooses people who are totally unworthy and, humanly speaking, may not have the most impressive gifts; through them, he does extraordinary things.
(para. 213)

I'm all for careful discernment and prudence, but our tendency today is to hang back too much, to be too cautious and careful, and maybe not to take risks and not to take ventures. When we do that, we cede territory to them, the worldly; we cede territory to the enemies of the Cross of Christ and to those who don't know God, and society continues to decline.
(para. 257)

---

211. Laurie: *How do you see the relationship between being a Christian and leadership?*

212. Aaron: Well, I think all Christians, in a sense, should think of themselves as leaders, not because we want to be in charge of things, but because we have been given an undeserved gift that, as Christians, we must try to share with others. Maybe a better way of saying that is that all of us should think of ourselves as apostles.

213. If you think about the people our Lord chose as the twelve apostles from a human point of view, they probably were not the people we would have chosen. This tax collector or this fisherman didn't have the typical CV [curriculum vitae] that a corporate leader or nonprofit leader would say, "Yes, this guy's got real leadership potential!" They would be, "Let's look around and find someone in the Roman Senate." Or "Let's look around and find someone in the Sanhedrin who kind of knows what they're doing." There's this paradoxical aspect of the Catholic Faith that our Lord chooses people

who are totally unworthy and, humanly speaking, may not have the most impressive gifts; through them, he does extraordinary things.

214. These twelve [apostles] managed to launch the process of evangelizing the whole world, which would have seemed impossible by any human calculation at the time. We take it for granted now, but if you stop and put yourself in their shoes and think about their social, political, and historical context, the idea that they could accomplish what they did would have sounded completely insane at the time. People probably did think that they were insane. All of them but one were martyred, and the last one was exiled on the island of Patmos.

215. So I think a Christian has a different notion of leadership than the world has. It doesn't begin with looking at our own talents and abilities. It's important; self-knowledge is important. I'm not trivializing that. And yes, at some point, you want to think about and discern what are the gifts that God has given you and how you can use them to serve the world. But before you do that, you have to develop the conviction in faith that God can do things through me that I could not accomplish through my own steam and abilities.

216. [Christian leadership] begins with the idea of the apostolate of the laity, that all of us are called to spread the Gospel by word and example, mostly through our everyday personal relationships: starting with our family, starting with our friends and acquaintances, starting with our colleagues at work, not by thumping on our Bible, not by preaching from a podium, and not typically by knocking on the door of strangers, but simply through our friendship and our relationship with them and our example - then looking for opportunities to speak with them about the great gift that God has given us.

217. That personal apostolate of friendship and confidence is, I think, the first aspect of leadership that all lay Catholics should think about and embrace. Beyond that, yes, there may be roles for you to head this or to direct that, and we should be ambitious, in the right sense of the term, for God. We should look for opportunities in society, or in the workplace, or in our neighborhood, or in our school to influence things for the better, to raise the spiritual temperature

around us and redirect those human activities toward God - either implicitly or explicitly.

218. But that has to begin with our own pursuit of a greater union with God. It has to begin, starting with our own personal relationships, of trying to help those that God has placed in our path to grow closer to him. And then, when we take on those positions of leadership, we should do so with a lot of humility and with the recognition that any good I do here is going to have to come from God. That means I need to redouble my prayer efforts. This means that I need to redouble my study of the Faith, Morals, and Social Teachings of the Catholic Church so I know what I'm doing and what I'm talking about. There are many well-meaning people out there who are just poorly formed in the Church's teachings and the doctrines of the Faith. And, if that's the case, you could be well-meaning, but you could end up doing more harm than good.

219. So, leadership needs to begin with humility. But then St. Josemaría Escrivá would talk about having a healthy superiority complex - this confidence, not in ourselves, but in the fact that we've been given a treasure, and we want to share that treasure with others. The Gospel is not ours; it does not belong to us. It was given to the Church of which we are members. We are all part of Christ's mystical body, so all of us have a responsibility to bring this treasure to the world. Not because we invented it, but precisely because we didn't; precisely because it was given to us. It was revealed to us by God, and that's where our confidence comes from. We can walk confidently into any environment knowing that we have something to offer there, not because we're brilliant or not because we're talented, but because through no merits of our own, we've been given something that maybe other people have not yet been exposed to. Woe to us if we don't share that with them!

220. **Laurie:** *One of the goals of Tepeyac Leadership Institute [TLIprogram.org] is to increase the engagement of the laity in leadership roles within their businesses and communities, particularly through a role of service such as being on a board of directors. You have served on several boards and committees. Can you tell us what boards you are currently on and what it's like to serve on a board?*

221. Aaron: I am currently on the board of the Seymour Institute for Black Church and Policy Studies [seymourinstitute.com], which was started by some black Pentecostals. They're sort of a think tank and policy nonprofit. The leadership there is very interested in Catholic Social Teaching because they recognize that their Pentecostalist tradition is not as theologically deep or rich when it comes to social teachings/moral teachings. They look to Catholics to help them in that regard, which is a beautiful thing, right? Ecumenically, there are strong areas of convergence and overlap: They care deeply about life issues. They care deeply about religious freedom. They care deeply about justice for the poor and for those who are marginalized. This particular group does a lot of work on reducing gang-related violence in the inner cities. They've worked in Boston with the leadership of the Catholic Church there to address some of these kinds of issues. It's been a joy to serve on that board because it's a chance to collaborate with Protestant brothers and sisters coming from a different sort of tradition of American Christianity, but there's a lot of, I would say, mutual respect for the work that both the Catholics and the Protestants are doing. So, that's been fun.

222. I got on that board because I was friends with the founders of the Seymour Institute. That's been an opportunity to collaborate with Christians and to learn from each other. The kind of evangelical fervor and bold proclamations of Black Pentecostalists is invigorating and Catholics have something to learn from that about getting out there and being daring and proclaiming our faith in Christ in a way that's not timid. I think they have something to learn from the rich intellectual tradition of Catholic thought about social and moral issues because they have the Bible, but the Bible alone doesn't necessarily answer all the contemporary questions that we're contending with now. You need a tradition of philosophy and theology informing your thinking there.

223. I'm also on the Advisory Board, not the Board of Directors, for a new initiative called Humanality [Humanality.org]. It is trying to help people, especially on college campuses, take a sane approach to engaging with technology screens - disengaging from the addictive nature of technology in order to spend more face-to-face time together and build communities around other activities so that we're not tethered to smartphones 24/7. That's an interesting project.

We've only had a few meetings, so, not a lot of experience with this yet.

224. I've served on the Board of Directors in the past for the local Catholic high school that my kids have gone to. Education is very important to me. That was a great opportunity to try to help a local educational institution. Again, I was invited to serve there because I'm friends with one of the founders of the school. He was looking for someone well formed in Catholic doctrine, Catholic Social Teaching and the Catholic Church's teachings on education. So, that was an opportunity to serve an institution that also helped my children.

225. I'm a believer that parents should not serve on the board of the school where their kid is currently attending, so I rolled off the board before my children got old enough to go to high school. There are legitimate differences of opinion on that question. People are usually motivated to serve on the board of a school because their children are benefiting. But I think there are some potential pitfalls to trying to run the show of an institution that you're directly benefiting from.

226. Laurie: *I like the idea of being there before your children go and setting up the best conditions.*

227. Aaron: Yes, I got to know the school. I could see the strengths and weaknesses of the school and make a contribution. I helped to recruit the current president of the school who's done a really good job there. I felt good about that. That was sort of my main contribution, helping to recruit the president of the school, who at the time was in Chicago at another school, and then roll off the board and let him do his thing. Three of our kids now have benefited - actually four - the fourth is a freshman this year.

228. Laurie: *It's important to know when to go on and when to come off boards because a lot of people don't know when to end an activity. Can you talk a little bit about that at all?*

229. Aaron: Yes. I think it's important to make room for new ideas. One of the things that can happen with institutions is that they can grow stale, not because the people leading them are not good people with good ideas but just because after a certain period of time, you made your mark and made the contribution that you're going to

make, and then you get into a little bit of a maintenance and tinkering mode. You're not necessarily bringing fresh energy or a new perspective. I think this goes for serving on boards and I think it goes for serving in various roles in institutions professionally.

230. I spent sixteen years in academia and in a medical school. The conventional wisdom in medical school was that a new chairman had five years to do something, and most of what they were going to do and most of what they were going to bring to a department would happen in the first couple of years. The idea there is a kind of life cycle to leadership is a valuable one. Different roles in different institutions may span different periods of time in which the natural life cycle of the leadership would run.

231. There are arguments to be made for institutional memory and having people stick around, maybe not in the highest leadership roles, but in supportive roles that have been in a place for thirty years and have seen people come and go. So, there's value to that as well. And there may be value in having someone in a kind of tenured leadership role for decades just to carry on a tradition or provide institutional stability.

232. But institutions, I think, tend to become sort of bureaucratized and sclerotic and require a kind of renewing and refreshing, sometimes just rediscovering their own traditions. It doesn't mean coming in and doing something totally new. It may mean just going deeper into who we are and what we're about and finding other new ways to express that: taking a tradition and digging into it in order to apply it to new circumstances. I think there's a dialectical sort of tension between tradition as kind of steady, solid, predictable, "This is how we've always done things," and reforming energies that want to try new things. Those things need to be in the right balance.

233. Laurie: *The creative tension of "Both/And."*

234. Aaron: Yes, yes, exactly. But I think there can be a tendency to want to hold on to power, prestige, or a title longer than you need to and not make way for new people. Not to pick on my parent's generation, but I think there's been a tendency among baby boomers, for example, to hang on to power and leadership politically in our society longer than they should and not make way for younger people and younger energy. And so, you see people in Congress and the Presidency that probably need to retire. There's nothing wrong with staying active and engaged as you age as long as you have the health and energy to do so but noticing when you're declining cognitively. Also, just notice when you've been here for decades, and maybe it's time to hang up the boxing gloves and let the younger people get in the ring and take a run at it. I think that's part of self-knowledge and humility.

235. Good leadership requires a certain level of detachment from power, which can become a bit of a drug for people. "What would I do with myself if I'm not in charge?" is not a good place for a leader to be. Maybe your leadership at this point is stepping aside and staying on in an advisory role, mentoring the next generation of leaders and bringing them along - what the psychologist Erik Erikson called Generativity, which he thought characteristic of the tasks to be accomplished later in life. You have a phase in life in which you're making your own contribution, and it's about, "What am I putting into the world?" or "What changes am I trying to make?" But too much of that can become sort of narcissistic. So, recognize when it's time for you to transition into, "Yes, I'm not going to be around forever, and I need to cultivate what the next generation is going to do in this profession."

236. Laurie: *What are the characteristics that we should look for in that next generation of leaders? If you're a mentor, what would you look for, or if you are a mentee and you want to develop certain skills, what would be those key characteristics?*

237. Aaron: Well, first of all, you have to have a certain level of professional excellence and know-how. It sounds basic to say it, but competence. You're not going to be in a position to lead an organization until you know the organization well, and you know the profession well, and you've achieved some level of excellence in that field. So, master the field. If it's education - become a really good educator or learn the skills necessary for effective administration. So, I think the first thing is competence. You have to be good at something.

238. You know there are people that want to lead before they've mastered whatever it is. "I want to be a leader in the world of science

and medicine." Well, are you a good scientist? Are you a good physician? Do you know cardiology really well? Do you provide really good patient care? Those are the first questions to ask. Or do you just want to be in charge of other people and tell them what to do? Are you just interested in power?

239. So, [pursue] professional excellence first but then [pursue] the ability to inspire other people. I think good leaders want to see other people thrive. I would use my own boss at EPPC, Ryan Anderson, as an example of that. To his great credit, the previous President of EPPC, Ed Whelen, demonstrated exactly what I described above by recognizing, before his abilities had declined, that he had reached the stage of life when it was time to make room for a younger leader with fresh energy and new ideas. Ryan, who succeeded him, was a successful public intellectual in his thirties. I think he published four or five books in his thirties, and then, when he hit forty, this opportunity came along to be president of EPPC. His wife sort of suggested, "Well, you've kind of made your mark, and maybe you can help people do what you have done. You can help other scholars do good research, get published, get their ideas out there, and sort of make their mark." That's kind of a generativity notion demonstrated by both Ed and Ryan in their leadership role. A good leader is less concerned about expanding his own CV and growing his own list of publications. Ryan is still writing and publishing, but most of his energy is focused on cultivating the other scholars at EPPC and wanting us to thrive.

240. Weak leaders tend to surround themselves with less-than-competent people because they're easier to control. Weak leaders want 'yes men' and 'yes women' - people who will just endorse whatever they want to do, support it, and block and tackle for them.

241. Strong leaders want to surround themselves with really competent people. If I'm the chairman of the psychiatry department, I get really excited to hire someone who's a better psychiatrist than I, who's a better researcher than I, who's a more accomplished whatever than I. I'm not threatened by that. Not, "Oh, maybe he's going to take my job," or "Maybe other people are going to recognize that he actually has better and more prestigious publications than I have." No, I rejoice in that because leadership is about cultivating excellence in other people rather than just exercising power, or

making myself look good, or being in charge, or having some title attached to my name.

242. Laurie: *How does a young person establish that respect in the workplace? When faced with conflict, how do they talk? How do they work?*

243. Aaron: I think young people should have a disposition of working quietly and effectively and letting the results speak for themselves; maintaining a certain humility and not needing to draw attention to themselves. If you just do the work really, really well, other people will notice. But if you start putting your work forward to show off, other people will get annoyed - quite rightly! So, pursue excellence and be excellent, but don't fall into the trap of trying to show off or get noticed. You don't have to. If you do really good work people will notice, but be humble about it; have a disposition that is open to learning even if you excel at something naturally.

244. I'll use academia [for an example] just because it's what I know. A young academic in her thirties quickly amasses more publications than someone more senior in the department. Okay, fine. But you still have something to learn from that person who is more senior. So, openness to learning, openness to mentorship and correction, and a non-defensive stance when you are corrected or redirected, I think, are signs of leadership potential.

245. Socrates was the only wise man in Athens because he realized he was not wise, whereas other people thought that they had wisdom. They didn't have that kind of Socratic humility - that wisdom of knowing that there's a lot that I don't know, even if it turns out I'm pretty good at something, kind of doing well, and maybe other people are noticing. But there's always someone who's better. Always [have a] learning mentality, always trying to grow and not trying to show off - letting the results of your work speak for themselves and assuming you have something to learn from everyone.

246. Laurie: *What about people who are struggling with seeing themselves as a leader, or they're struggling even to find purpose or a reason to lead? They're just not sure what they should put their energy and time into. Do you have any words of wisdom for people who may be struggling with that?*

247. Aaron: Well, I think it's hard to lead something effectively unless you really care about it and have a passion for it. So, if you're struggling in that regard, one question is, "Do you really have a passion for this thing?"

248. Laurie: *How do they find that? How do they find that passion? There are a lot of young people that are kind of lost.*

249. Aaron: I think you have to try things. I think you have to stretch yourself and put yourself out there. Many people discover that they're good at something because they step off the ledge and dare to try it. Someone invites them and they've never thought about joining this group, joining this board or contributing to this thing. They may think, "I don't really know what I'm doing here. I don't really know what I'm talking about, but I'm going to try it. I'm going to sort of dive in. I'm going to have a beginner's mind that's open to learning and I'm going to try to get to know the other people involved." In many cases, I think they discover, "Wow, yes, this is really neat! And I'm good at this aspect of this thing. Maybe I'm not the person who talks and intervenes a lot in the conversations, but I'm really good at staying organized and getting certain kinds of action items done because I'm a very orderly person, and I can prioritize. That's how I make my contribution to this thing."

250. I think a willingness to try things and to step out of your comfort zone is important. You never grow if you don't stretch yourself and make yourself, at times, a little bit uncomfortable.

251. Laurie: *I'm thinking back to where you talked about the boards that you're on, where you're recognized for your competencies, your expertise in terms of the medical and the Catholic Social Teaching, but you were open to stepping off the ledge and being on the board for organizations that you wouldn't necessarily...*

252. Aaron: Yes! The Seymour Institute is a good example. I think there are two Catholics now on the board. But when I first joined, I was the only Catholic. [I thought], "This is great, but" you know, it's this, "Are these people going like me?" Right? "I'm not one of them." But of course, they're just beautiful people, and they were so welcoming. So that was interesting and fun.

253. I've served on that board a long time. I think initially, I told Gene Rivers [the President of Seymour] because of time constraints, I'm only going to do this for three years. I think we're probably pushing eight years now. I can't remember exactly when I joined that board, but it's been a while. I just like it. It's fun, and they're good people.

254. So yes, sometimes, you need to get a little bit outside of your comfort zone, and then you're going to learn something. Inner-city gang-related violence was never an issue that I knew about. It's not that I didn't care about it. I just didn't know much about it. How would you tackle something like this? I had no idea. I'm a kid from the suburbs! But I've learned by serving on that board. There is Seymour's ten-point program. How do you go into a community and engage with local church leadership, local community leadership, and local police and try to address a really, really, really hard problem, a really intractable problem? There are actually ways to do it, but it's difficult.

255. So there's only one way to learn something, and that's to go places where you don't know things.

256. **Laurie:** *That is a great example of being willing to put yourself out there. Can you talk a little more about the benefits of taking risks and going out of your comfort zone when following Christ?*

257. **Aaron:** Yes, in contemporary society especially, Catholics have to be daring. We don't abandon prudence and, in some professional contexts, we have to pick our battles. Maybe this is not the hill I want to die on. Maybe God is calling me to focus more on this issue over there and not lose my job because I am trying to fight this other issue over here. I'm all for careful discernment and prudence, but our tendency today is to hang back too much, to be too cautious and careful, and maybe not to take risks and not to take ventures. When we do that, we cede territory to them, the worldly; we cede territory to the enemies of the Cross of Christ and to those who don't know God, and society continues to decline.

258. I remember reading a homily by Saint John Henry Newman in college. I believe it was essentially asking the question, "What have you ventured for Christ?" Imagine that everything you believe about the Christian Faith turned out not to be true and look at your life.

What would you have? What would you have ventured? Given your Catholic Faith, what would be different in your life if you didn't believe any of this stuff? It's a good question to ask ourselves, "What have we ventured for Christ? What have we risked for this proposition of Faith?"

259. Because if the answer is, "Well, you know, if I didn't believe in God, if I didn't believe in the Catholic Faith, I would more or less conduct myself the way I'm conducting myself now." That might be an indication that perhaps we're not being daring enough. Perhaps we're not venturing enough to try to advance the kingdom of God.

260. Laurie: *Interesting. Where do you think there's the greatest need now for the lay Catholic?*

261. Aaron: Everywhere. There's no sector of human society where Catholics do not belong.

262. I would say certainly education if you're inclined to get involved in education and in some respects, the earlier, the better. So, early education is very important and helping to support families in the work of forming children in the Catholic Faith is very important.

263. But there's no sector from business to entertainment to medicine, to public service and politics, to education, to the world of nonprofits and NGOs [Non-governmental Organizations] where Catholics don't belong and where Catholics, faithful Catholics, couldn't have a tremendous impact. I think God needs a handful of people in every sector of society to help establish the peace of Christ in the kingdom of Christ. And so, it doesn't matter if you're a street sweeper or a surgeon; God needs you there, wherever you're called, and you need to have a sense of responsibility that you're doing something great.

264. I heard this anecdote just last week in the homily that my pastor gave where President Kennedy, back during the space program, visited NASA and asked one of the janitors working at NASA, "What are you doing?" And the man responded, "I'm helping to put a man on the moon!" Just a wonderful anecdote about how we should think about our professional work. You can read that from a supernatural perspective, as well. The Uber driver, or the person cleaning the

toilets, or the Prime Minister - it shouldn't matter: "What are you doing?" "I'm trying to sanctify my work, and I'm helping to advance the kingdom of God."

265. Laurie: *Yes, sometimes there are recognition and awards - like the St. Juan Diego Leadership for the World and other awards you've received - but there are also intangible aspects of how you contribute.*

266. Aaron: That's right - the most important contributions! I tried to say this in my [St. Juan Diego Leadership for the World] award remarks - there are saints among us, and they're typically not the people receiving the awards. I'd be happy if you quoted some of those lines from that talk [see Appendix] because I really do believe that the real saints are people that we would never know, and from a supernatural perspective, the people doing the most good at advancing the kingdom of God.

267. Most are probably hidden; they're the disabled person who has a profound interior joy when he receives Communion, even if he's nonverbal, and requires the total care of his parents. He may be the holiest person in your parish; he may have the highest place in heaven. God's logic is upside down, and Jesus was serious when he said, "But many who are first will be last, and the last will be first." [Mathew 19:30] So that guy may be the real leader in the parish. He may be drawing more Grace down upon the other parishioners than the pastor who gives eloquent homilies or the highly successful, visible personality who receives awards from Catholic groups that happens to attend that parish. That's not God's actual way of doing things. So the people who receive the awards need to be most careful about the danger of pride and being self-satisfied and to recognize that the kid in your parish with Down Syndrome is probably a lot closer to Jesus than you are. So, you have a lot of work to do! Obviously, I'm grateful for the St. Juan Diego Leadership for the World Award from TLI. I don't want to insult the people who are doing these things. That's great. Recognize good Catholic professionals out there trying to do good work; hold up examples for others to emulate in professional life. All of that is wonderful, but let's keep in mind the perspective of the Gospel.

268. Let's go back and really meditate upon the Beatitudes and what our Lord is saying there. We'll recognize that the greatest sacrifices, the greatest acts of Christian leadership, are probably hidden, and they're probably done by people that no one ever takes any notice of and no one ever sees.

269. Laurie: *As you've mentioned, saints are sometimes not the ones you expect, and the leaders are not necessarily the ones that are in the news. But they are leaders. So, this gives an opportunity to shine a spotlight on some of those people that are examples.*

270. Aaron: Yes, my friend, Father Rick Sera, who was a priest here in the Diocese of Orange, passed away recently. He died of cancer. I've known him for years. Several years ago, someone in Rome reached out asking [recommendations for], I think, the position of spiritual director at the North American College in Rome, something like that. They wanted someone ideally who's a priest and who also had training in psychology. Father Rick had both a PhD in psychology and his theological training as a priest. I thought, "He's ideal," and I mentioned that to the person who reached out to me, and they said, "Can you see if he's interested? Sounds like a great candidate!"

271. So, I reached out to Father Rick, and he admitted, "Yes, that sounds like my dream job as a priest, actually. But I have to stay here and care for my disabled brother who has schizophrenia." So, he passed on it. He continued to care for his brother, who has schizophrenia, until he died. That's leadership, even though he didn't get the prestigious leadership position at the prestigious seminary in Rome. He's an 'ordinary parish priest' here. That's real leadership to me.

272. Laurie: *Yes. Sacrificial servant leadership. Any other inspirational leaders that are living that have impacted your life?*

273. Aaron: Oh, that's a good question. Let me think…

274. My friend Dr. Jay Bhattacharya, who's the new head of the NIH, is a very good man. I just have tremendous respect for him. He was receiving an award at LMU [Loyola Marymount University]. Part of that was giving a lecture and he was allowed to invite someone to give a twenty-minute commentary on his lecture after his talk. He

invited me, so I went there, and they gave me a very generous honorarium, especially for academia. They usually don't give large speaking stipends at universities. We have tight, tight budgets, especially for a twenty-minute talk. I was like, "Wow, that's a really generous honorarium." I saw Jay six months later; we were in Rome together speaking to a group of Catholic politicians. Somehow the LMU event came up in his talk. [Afterwards] I said, "Yes, they gave me a really generous stipend." And he said, "Oh, yes, that was the award money. I told them to give it to you because you lost your job, whereas I still have my job at Stanford." He never would have said anything about that had I not brought it up to him. That's just the kind of person he is, so very humble, very generous, very self-effacing and very faithful. He's a Protestant Christian but when we were in Rome, he went to Mass with me every day, which was great. So, I just have a lot of respect for Jay. I think he's a real leader, and I'm glad to see that he's been tapped for an important leadership position in science and medicine.

275. There are scholars whose work I'm very fond of. Dr. Iain McGilchrist is a really interesting scholar who writes on the interface of philosophy and science. He's doing important work. My friend Dr. Matthias Desmet is another scholar whose work I admire a lot and who has written about the psychology of totalitarianism.

276. Most of the leaders that come to mind would not be people that the readers are going to know. They're not doing sort of big, publicly known, prestigious things, but they're leaders in their own small way, in their own sphere of influence.

277. **Laurie:** *You might say they are leading a good life! Along those lines, what do you consider the most important part of life, or what has brought you the most joy?*

278. **Aaron:** Well, the things that have brought me the most joy are relationships. Certainly, the Trinitarian God is a relation of three divine persons; God is in His own inner life - relationships. And He created us to be in relationships with others.

279. I think if you ask most people at the end of their life what was most important to them, they would talk about their relationships as they're facing their own mortality. It's not going to be how much

money I made. It's not going to be how many awards I got, or how many books I sold, or whatever. What's most important to them is going to be their relationships. Their greatest regrets are going to be broken relationships or relationships that perhaps they were not able to reconcile.

280. So, first and foremost, my relationship with God and then, second, my relationship with my family and my friends, and my colleagues and my coworkers. Those have been the sources of greatest joy and edification, and there's plenty of psychological research that bears this out.

281. There was a famous study called the Harvard Grant Study, which followed people out for several decades (it started in the 1930s) from their college years all the way through to their death. George Vaillant, a psychologist, was one of the lead authors of that study. I brought him to UC Irvine to give a talk several years ago, and he was talking about the findings of that study. His conclusion for that study was basically the meaning of life, the way to find happiness is through love.

282. Basically, the quality of your relationships is the most predictive thing for health, human flourishing and happiness. However we might want to try to assess that using the metrics of psychology or psychiatry, insofar as we can measure something like happiness or human flourishing, it seems to be related to the quality of people's relationships and their capacity to give and receive love.

283. The people I treat who suffer the most and have been wounded the most are from a lack of love, usually in their early years. The wounds that result from that are so profound and so deep that they can only be healed by God's Love and by God's Grace.

284. So that's what we're made for, and it may sound cliché, but it's nonetheless true: the meaning of life is love and charity - love of God and love of neighbor. Which is, you know, more or less what our Lord tried to tell us.

285. The last thing I'll say is I'm not a fountain of wisdom, but for what it's worth, these are my thoughts in my current stage of life.

APPENDIX

Aaron Kheriaty
St. Juan Diego Leadership for the World Award Remarks

The Hour of the Laity Conference, TLI Inc.
November 9, 2024

288. There are saints among us. They are not the ones receiving awards (all due respect to my friends, you and I are a work in progress). These saints among us include the old man quietly praying the rosary while he rides the city bus to the market. They include the young woman who forgoes brilliant career opportunities to care for her disabled child. They include the girl dying of cancer and offering her pain for her brother to return to the faith.

289. There is suffering in store for us, for suffering is inevitable in a fallen world. But that is good. For in suffering, we can find the Cross, and in the Cross, we find God's love for us. Suffering with Christ is co-redemptive. I anticipate in our lifetime a battle for the family, a battle for the dignity of the human person. We may suffer as we fight for good to prevail.

290. We will be outnumbered, but God will prevail by means of our prayers: the rosary will be our weapon, and Our Lady of the Rosary will lead us to victory as she led the Christian fleet at the great Battle of Lepanto. This battle will have its martyrs. Ours may be a "white martyrdom" involving personal attacks, slander, professional persecution, reputational harm, and other sacrifices that will often fall short of giving one's life. To survive these attacks with our souls intact, we will need to care more about the good opinion of God than the opinion of others.

291. Our task today is to find God in the Cross: to meditate more deeply on the details of Christ's Passion. I want to recommend to you a brief prayer that will be very helpful here. It's a simple aspiration that you can repeat many times a day: *Doce me passionem Tuam,* which translates, "teach us your suffering" or "teach us your passion." *Doce me passionem Tuam.* We have all read the Gospels, but perhaps we do not yet really know Christ's Passion. We must learn it. He must teach us. We must live it more deeply in order to find him.

292. Paradoxically, it is in suffering that we find freedom. It is in Christ's passion - with all its horrors, all the blood, the dirt, the grit, the sweat, the tears - it is there that we find peace. Interior freedom and interior peace are not found in politics. They are not found in elections, as important as these things are. Freedom and peace are found only in the Cross of Christ. There

is no Easter Sunday without Good Friday. *Doce me passionem Tuam,* "Teach me your suffering, Lord."

293. We have examples of this in the saints, especially in the martyrs. Think, for example, of Saint Thomas More as depicted in the film *A Man for All Seasons.* I spoke yesterday about how he was a martyr for marriage, for the unity of the Church, and even for freedom of speech.

294. I recommend to you also, if you have not seen it, Terrence Malik's film, *A Hidden Life,* about another martyr, Blessed Franz Jaggerstatter. Franz was an ordinary husband, father, and farmer in Austria when Germany invaded during WWII. He was conscripted into the German army and was willing to fight. But what he was NOT willing to do was to swear the required Oath of Fidelity to Adolf Hitler. His friends and neighbors, the mayor of his town, and even the well-meaning parish priest pleaded with him to be reasonable: just sign it, they told him, even if you don't mean it. Just a pinch of incense to the Emperor, and then they'll leave you alone. But Franz could not do this in good conscience. In one pivotal scene in the film, he is being beaten senseless in prison by a prison guard. The guard looks down at him and says, "Just sign it, and you'll be free." Bloodied, bruised, and unable to stand, Franz looks up through his black eye and beaten face and says, "But I already am free…"

295. If we unite ourselves to Christ on the Cross, there will always remain something in us - the most important part of us - that nothing else can touch, that no malice or evil can ever destroy. In his last letter from prison, Franz wrote, "Although I am writing with my hands in chains, this is still much better than if my will were in chains."

296. Thank you for this undeserved award, which really belongs to all the hidden saints among us. I will try to live up to what it signifies - courage and leadership - keeping in mind the words of St. Josemaría Escrivá that "all our fortitude is on loan."

Doce me passionem Tuam. Thank you, and God bless you.

We hope you enjoyed this book.

Please consider supporting our efforts by learning about, praying for, or financially supporting Tepeyac Leadership, Inc.

Please visit:

TLIprogram.org
THLconference.org

www.ingramcontent.com/pod-product-compliance
Lightning Source LLC
Chambersburg PA
CBHW071341130626
46556CB00004B/1977